CONFESSION OF A TERRORIST!

Musings on Bangladesh Liberation War

AbulKalam M. Shamsuddin

IP-6 Research Inc.
Baltimore, MD, USA
www.iP-6.net

International Standard Book Number (ISBN) 978-984-33-2219-7

Copyright: 2010 by AbulKalam M. Shamsuddin

All rights reserved. No parts of this book may be reproduced in any form or by any means without the prior written consent of the Author excepting brief quotes.

E-mail: research@ip-6.net

First printed in February 2011
Printed in United States of America

Available from Amazon.com and other fine retailers

US$ 19.71

*To Dr Maj (Retd) Akhtar Ahmed Beer Protik
who gave me the honor and privilege of serving
the freedom fighters of Bangladesh, who
through his confidence in me and his valor,
dedication, patriotism and above all self-respect
had influenced my life immensely*

And

*To all those who have contributed to the
eventual liberation of our homeland
no matter how small or big that had been*

FOREWORDS

More than four decades have passed since the liberation war of Bangladesh, but few accounts of the day-to-day roles of the tens of thousands of freedom fighters at the war fronts are available. Professor Shamsuddin, who himself suspended his own joining of the lucrative medical training in U.S. medical services system to join the liberation war, gives a detailed account of the glorious roles many unknown heroes played in the liberation of Bangladesh from his first experience as a freedom fighter. Instead of relying on any secondary sources, he diligently and objectively narrated, from his own personal experience, the various roles played by many unknown active participants, including doctors, nurses, and other volunteers.

The book describes the moment of triumphs as well as temporary setbacks in the course of the liberation war. But the spirit and hope of independence of our country from the yoke of imperialist Pakistan were always present among all these freedom fighters, while facing the enemies in the front, which resulted in speedy attainment of the freedom. Without such a vivid and objective account of the sacrifices by tens of thousands of unknown freedom fighters, no true history of the liberation can be known to our posterior generations who must learn from our glorious liberation struggle.

Ruhul Amin, Ph. D.
Senior Faculty, Johns Hopkins University,
Baltimore, MD, USA
Former Acting Director of Institute of Urban
Research, Morgan State University and
Former Associate Professor, Chittagong
University, Bangladesh
July 31, 2010

TABLE OF CONTENTS

Chapter		Page
	Preface....................................	1
1	Rendezvous................................	9
2	Jungle Camps.............................	56
3	Hunting Trip...............................	92
4	Tent Hospital	116
5	Bamboo Hospital........................	141
6	Target 6.....................................	174
7	Dream Come True	220
8	Longest Month...........................	255
	Epilogue...................................	295
	Introduction to Characters.............	303

PREFACE

Who is a terrorist?

Fighting for the Zionist state of Israel against the British, under the command of Menachem Begin, Irgun the Zionist militia bombed the British administrative headquarters at the King David Hotel in Jerusalem, where 91 people, including British officers and troops as well as Arab and Jewish civilians were killed on 22 July 1946. *"Many believe that the attacks carried out under Begin's leadership of a Jewish militia, the Irgun, helped hasten the British withdrawal from mandate Palestine, and the establishment of the Jewish state of Israel"* (http://terrorism.about.com/od/groupsleader1/p/MenachemBegin.htm). Labeling him a Terrorist, British MI5 announced a £10,000 bounty on his head; that became irrelevant when Begin the terrorist became the Prime Minister of Israel! He went on to receive the Nobel Prize for Peace and so did other fellow former terrorists – Yaser Arafat and Nelson Mandela! But why did a member of the

Confession of a Terrorist!
Preface

Nobel Peace Prize Committee resign over the accord of the Prize to Yaser Arafat and not others?! Is that because Arafat was a terrorist but Begin and Mandela not?! Does one get to choose their favorite terrorist of the year?!

Like all other free people on this planet, the history of India too is replete with our struggle for freedom during the various periods of its occupation by outsiders. I suppose India had an added attraction; starting from Alexander the Great to the Mongols and Mughols, the Persians and in later period most European colonial powers had invaded and occupied our land. Very few if any occupier leave their newly snatched land voluntarily, much less peacefully. Even Mahatma Gandhi could not have kicked the Brits out of our homeland solely by his non-violent movement; there were many other factors that helped their ouster, not least of which is *Netajee* Shuvash Chandra Bose's armed struggle. One of the first, if not the first Bengali to express his wishes was of course Khudiram Bose. To us, he was a hero, and still is. To the occupying British colonial authorities: a terrorist. And so was Menachem Begin. In a sad and ironic twist of fate, the Zionist state that Begin the Terrorist had help create has been battling the Palestinian "terrorists" ever since!

Confession of a Terrorist!
Preface

When the Pakistani military started to massacre innocent Bengali civilians in East Pakistan and terrorized the entire nation, it was not a crime in the eye of other colonial occupiers. Worse, the Nixon administration of USA supported it! Bengalis are Buddhists, Christians, Hindus and Moslems; and none were spared. Paradoxically the minority were the major recipients of Pakistani military's wrath. So when over 10 million Bengalis were forced out of their homeland, another 3 million or so of at least 4 different religious affiliations were slaughtered and 400,000 women raped, why did it not matter to the "civilized" world?

As though hypocrisy had no limit, just 9 days after ordering an additional 30,000 troops in Afghanistan to battle the "terrorists" there, in accepting the premature Nobel Peace Prize, US President Barack Hussein Obama stated on 10 December 2009 "A nonviolent movement could not have halted Hitler's armies." He continued "To say that force is sometimes necessary is not a call to cynicism; it is a recognition of history." (http://www.msnbc.msn.com/id/34358659/ns/politics-white_house). Like Hitler, Mr. President, to put it in your words Sir, would non-violent movement have stopped the genocide by Pakistani Military? Sir, you said "Negotiations cannot convince al-

Confession of a Terrorist!
Preface

Qaida's leaders to lay down their arms," Sheikh Mujibur Rahman, the Prime Minister-elect did not have the privilege of your wisdom, he was negotiating all the while the Pakistani army was building up their forces in Bangladesh every night. The Bengali nation had no choice but side with your wisdom and fought, yet opposed by your predecessor President Richard M. Nixon. Why is force justified by one party and not the other? Who and how is it determined as to which party has the right to use force? It is odd, all occupiers and colonialists have used force in one form or another and at one time or another to terrorize and control the populace; but it is politically incorrect for the victims to think of, much less speak of armed resistance against the very powers that have through terror and brute force illegally occupied their mother/fatherland lest they are branded as "terrorist." Why so? Is it because "might is right?" Our predecessors, Khudiram Bose, Teetumeer, Shurjo Sen, Pritilata Waddedar, *Netajee* Shuvash Chandra Bose taught us to resist and protest the unwelcome and illegal occupation with force or "acts of terrorism" to our enemy– like give them a "taste of their own medicine." The prescription seems to have worked everywhere: in contemporary time it has worked in Bangladesh and South Africa as examples.

Confession of a Terrorist!
Preface

On the subject of medicine and terrorism, I was a final year medical student who along with the rest of the Bengali nation was terrorized by the Pakistani military. The people of Bangladesh answered them with doses of their own medicine; fair enough?! All I wanted was my motherland to be free; so I served those who fought for that freedom – Freedom Fighters to us and terrorists to our enemy forces, the best way I could.

Not knowing whether I will even survive, let alone be back in a free Bangladesh, I had started to write down my experience and observations on a daily basis in a journal or diary. I had collected each and every shrapnel and bullet that I had personally extracted from the wounded Freedom Fighters. After I returned to Dhaka on 16 January 1972, I had left the diary and my collections at the then my wife's parents' house for convenience. Needless to say, that after their mysterious disappearance several weeks later, I was devastated; I had lost my most beloved and precious of all possessions ever.

Humbly serving the Freedom Fighters was my greatest privilege and honor, independence of my homeland was my reward. I never felt the urge to write about that experience; being severely disheartened by the loss of those memorabilia made

Confession of a Terrorist!
Preface

me even more uninterested despite Dr. Major Akhtar Ahmed *Beer Protik*'s repeated suggestions that I do; I simply did not have the motivation anymore.

Enter Dr. Abdul Baten, a young man from the district of Borishal in coastal Bangladesh, who had done his MD and PhD at the Peoples' Friendship University and DI Ivanovsky Institute of Virusology in Moscow, Russia respectively. In 1988 he joined my laboratory at the University of Maryland School Of Medicine to work on IP-6 & Inositol (www.ip-6.net). Baten was a hardworking intelligent person; his modesty belied the fact that he was a Freedom Fighter (a local Commander) who was seriously wounded in combat following a fierce firefight with the Pakistan army. Though this past of his was unbeknown to me, we nevertheless developed a very cordial, mutually respectful relationship during his tenure in my research laboratory. In commemoration of the victory day (*Bijoy Dibosh*) of 16 December, in November of 2009 he invited me to contribute an article in a magazine he was especially publishing. My gratitude is to Freedom Fighter Dr. Abdul Baten for his inspiration in composing the book, for without that I would not have done it.

Confession of a Terrorist!
Preface

Once I started to compose, I began to recall a lot of events; but I also had forgotten the names of a few people and had consulted the book *"Baar Baar Feerey Jai"* (I go back again and again) by Dr. Major Akhtar Ahmed *Beer Protik*; I am thankful to him for that too. This memory loss prompted me to hurry up and save that information before senile dementia or worse, Alzheimer's disease robs all of them away. My gratitude also goes to my dear friend Anna-Maria Delinasiou whose comments have been very helpful. My very dear friend Dr A. Q. M. Mahmood who too served our Freedom Fighters as a medical officer has elephant-like memory helped me recollect many events and gave me constructive critiques. I am indebted to him also for his kind donation of photographs; many of the pictures in this book are from his collection.

The amount of help and kindness we received from people of India, fellow Bengalis and non-Bengali's alike, during our struggle for the independence of our motherland is unfathomable. It is my personal belief that without their open-armed acceptance of us, our refugees, providing us with food, roofs over our head, all the other necessities and more, it would have been nearly impossible to achieve our goal. Innocent civilians in Indian border towns were terrorized only because they sheltered us; the

Confession of a Terrorist!
Preface

entire Indian nation was subjected to a special tax to help defray the cost of aiding over 10 million refugees, not including over 120,000 Freedom Fighters. Last but not the least, the brave members of Indian military gave their lives for us. I owe India, its people and its government, especially under Mrs. Indira Gandhi an eternal debt of gratitude for their enormous generosity to and sacrifice for our fellow countrymen and me personally.

Here is an account of how I strived to make my humble contribution:

A. K. M. Shamsuddin

CHAPTER 1

RENDEZVOUS WITH THE TERRORISTS

TO THE JUNGLES OF TRIPURA, INDIA

Apology

es, I am guilty; I am guilty of treating young men, many of them in their teens (boys) for severe malaria, devastating diarrhea, and other ailments. Yes, I am also guilty of taking *your* bullets and bombshell fragments from their wounds and patching them up so that they could go back and fight you again, and again for their freedom, for the independence of their homeland.

Confession of a Terrorist!
Chapter 1   Rendezvous

This would have been my statement to the victorious Pakistan Army *if* they would have crushed the Bengali Nation and I was detained. But fortunately for me and fellow Bengalis, fate was not that kind to Pakistan…

On that apocalyptic night of 25 March 1971, I wanted to fight the Pakistan army. From our house in Tezgaon Dhaka, beginning about 22:00 Hrs. I could see the columns of Pakistan Army and their torching of houses and shops along the road. Our neighborhood was almost desolate; most able-bodied men, women and children had left for their villages for safety. Two or three of my next-door-neighbors, men in their early thirties, government employees who had to report to office stayed back. We became very apprehensive about what was going on or what will happen, for the air was thick and smelled of trouble; it was calm before the storm. Our house was about 200 m south of Indra Road that ran parallel to the main avenue towards the Songshod Bhobon (House of Parliament) from the Airport Road, at Farm Gate[1]. This was the only

---

[1] The current day *Sher-e-Bānglā Nagar* used to be a very large Experimental Agricultural Farm (approximately 2x3 km) between the Airport Road on the east, Mirpur Road on the west and Indra Road on the south with an Agricultural College roughly around where the *Songshod Bhobon* (Parliament) is now. Besides being an agricultural farm, it had exotic trees and poultry. The present day park between the westbound

Confession of a Terrorist!
Chapter 1   Rendezvous

way the military could come to the city from the Cantonment. During those days, that was the northern-most edge of the city of Dhaka; the entire lot from Indra Road to our house was an empty but uneven turf, part of which was level ground where we played. A 1.5 m high wall on the southern boundary of the sports ground separated our house from the open field. This boundary wall acted as a defensive shield allowing us to see what was happening on the other side without being seen or taking the bullets. By 22:30 Hrs. we could hear machinegun fire; bullets were flying past, fortunately a meter or so above the wall and our head. A man who was too naive went close to Indra Road and felled by the bullets; alas, his curiosity cost him his life. The night-sky was lit up bright red in fire, first to the east in the Farm Gate area where there were a few small businesses (sweet shops) owned or presumed to be owned by the minority Hindus, mixed with other shops owned by non-Hindus. A loud boom and the sky was red, flames and smoke were billowing; then there were more booms and pretty

---

and eastbound Manik Mia Avenue had cinnamon and bay-leaf trees; as children we would occasionally pickup a bay-leaf and snip-off the bark of cinnamon trees to enjoy the taste. At the entrance to this farm on the intersection of Airport Road and eastbound Manik Mia Avenue was a wrought-iron gate, hence the name of the area Farm Gate. In the 1960's the Pakistan government developed the farm to "Second Capital" by which name it was known till the independence of Bangladesh.

Confession of a Terrorist!
Chapter 1   Rendezvous

soon the southern and western skies joined the eastern part in its fiery display; the northern sky over the military cantonment was exceptionally clear. All we could hear throughout the entire night was the sounds of machine guns, tank fires and bombs. I do not know anyone in Dhaka who could sleep that night or not felt terrorized.

It was obvious that the Pakistani military was targeting the minorities, the intellectuals, the students, the nationalists irrespective of whether they were politicians or not, and anyone who were in their sight that night… they wanted to terrorize the Bengali nation and break its backbone forever so that we could be permanently enslaved to a submissive colony. Naturally, our minority Christian (Roman Catholics) neighbors had even more reasons to be afraid and came to our house in total panic. Our cook Mannan and I were the only ones living in the house as I had sent the rest of my family to the village in Comilla, about 160 km to the southeast, a couple of weeks prior. But I did not think that it would be safe to shelter my neighbors in the main house; they would have been immediately detected and murdered. The men were coping with their fright by heavy drinking of cheap alcohol that you could smell even without them talking; the Pakistan army would not need to interrogate them;

Confession of a Terrorist!
Chapter 1   Rendezvous

with their fanatic intolerance for minorities combined with the smell of booze, it would be an open invitation to slaughter them. Somewhat semidetached was a study-room for my siblings which could be locked from outside. I thought that if I put my neighbors in this room and locked the door from outside, it would be less likely to arouse the suspicion of the Pakistani military especially since there were none else in the main house. So my terrified and terrorized neighbors spent the rest of the night of the 25th March – about a dozen of them, women and children included huddled up in that 3x4 m small room in total darkness with a large padlock hanging outside the only door.

Rebirth

The next 60+ hours were demoralizing. There was a curfew; anyone seen on the street was to be shot at sight. The round-the-clock curfew lasted till the 27th; it was lifted for a mere two hours to 'kindly' allow us to get our groceries and other bare necessities. Gradually the 'humanitarian' gesture of allowing us to live like human being was extended. The mighty Pakistani military machine has been ruthlessly killing innumerable number of my fellow countrymen; eyewitnesses who were more

Confession of a Terrorist!
Chapter 1 Rendezvous

careful than our unfortunate neighbor who got shot, kept on feeding us one horror story after another – the Pakistani military has indeed broken our backbone. Still, not to give up hope, I like everyone else had my ear glued to the radio and my hand turning the frequency-knob searching for radio-stations for any news to bring back the life in moribund me. As if it was a miracle: a faint voice with static noises in the background revived me and I suppose the rest of Bengali nation[2]; it was "Major"

---

[2] Bānglā stands for the land of Bengal or the language spoken in the present day Bangladesh (*desh* means land or country) and the Indian state of West Bengal. The 'superior' British colonialists could not pronounce Bānglā (!) and Anglicized it to Bengal (for the land) or Bengali for the language (Bānglā) or the people (Bāngāli). Bengal that included the current day Bangladesh which used to be East Bengal plus the Indian State of West Bengal had an area of 489,500 sq. km with a population of approximately 80 million in early 1900. To curtail the political agitation arising in the East, the then Viceroy of India Lord Curzon had divided Bengal into East and West Bengal in 1905 over mass protests; it was announced on 19 July and took effect on 16 October. In 1947 during the Independence of India, West Bengal joined India while, East Bengal with Moslem majority joined overwhelmingly Moslem West Pakistan 1,600 km away across India as East Pakistan. Civilization in greater Bengal dates back to approximately 4,000 BCE when it was settled by Dravidians, Tibeto-Burman and Austro-Asiatic peoples. The word Bānglā probably arose from the *Bāng* tribe of the Dravidians who settled there. Sadly, Bengalis had neither been able to rule themselves for long, nor did they allow foreigners to rule them for an extended period

Confession of a Terrorist!
Chapter 1 Rendezvous

Zia who proclaimed the independence of Bangladesh under the direction of *Bongo Bondhu* (Friend of Bengal) Sheikh Mujibur Rahman! And the message was repeated time and time again mingled with patriotic songs. Under his command *Mukti Bahini* (Freedom Fighters or the Resistance) was fighting the Pakistani military and he appealed for us to join.

The following few days and weeks were confusing: the Pakistani military said that they crushed us "the miscreants" and the *Mukti Bahini* state how many Pakistanis they had killed. But one thing I know for sure that several of my friends, relatives and neighbors were slaughtered by the Pakistani military. My classmate and friend Jogodish Haldar, a Hindu - one of the most benign persons on earth was rumored to have been killed[3]. My high school

---

(http://en.wikipedia.org/wiki/Bangladesh; http://en.wikipedia.org/wiki/1905_Partition_of_Bengal). Dhaka (again Anglicized by the British colonialist to Dacca!) had been the capital of East Bengal.

Sheikh Mujibur Rahman was the leader of Awami League whose party won the majority of seats in the Pakistani Parliament, therefore the Prime Minister-Elect, but was denied the position by ruling Pakistani Military triggering the events of 25th March 1971.

[3] Fortunately, rumor of Jogodish's death was just that - a rumor; I found out lately that he had managed to escape to Kolkata, India.

Confession of a Terrorist!
Chapter 1   Rendezvous

classmate and friend Anwarul Alim, and his twin brother Selim, both Muslims, were executed at the Ferry port on their way of escaping to their village.

Front: Hajra(1), Razzaque(2), Nuru, Moshtaque, Nuruzzaman, Mannan, Nazmul, Alim, Matin, Quamruzzaman(3), Shamsuddin
Middle: Nazimul, Daniel, Alauddin(4), Halim, Shiraj, Shafique(5), Mizan, Huda, Shahid, Ali Hosen, Shamsur Rahman, Jashim
Back: Nur Ahmad (caretaker), Kabir, Mofiz, Amjad(6), Kader, Amin, Kamal, Khairul, Rabib, Khaled, Rashid, Hafiz

My high school class picture of 1963. The smiling rather happy and jovial Anwarul Alim (with glasses) is fourth from the right on the front row (myself at far right with a stack of books).

In this world full of bullies at every level, being physically lanky and somewhat weak I suppose I compensated by developing mental strength. I became determined to fight the mighty Pakistan military; but how and where? I have heard of many of my friends and acquaintances leaving home to join

Confession of a Terrorist!
Chapter 1   Rendezvous

Mukti Bahini and also heard of many who were caught by the Pakistani military and summarily executed. I certainly did not want to step into the trap and be killed by them; for a dead patriot is a useless patriot, nothing more than a corpse.

My betrothed Daliah's father's younger brother was elected as Member of the Parliament belonging to Awami League, the party of Sheikh Mujibur Rahman the Prime Minister-Elect of Pakistan who is now in Pakistani jail. One of Daliah's brothers - Shelley was also involved in student politics aligned with Awami League like his uncle. He and two of his friends, Ulfat and Manzoor decided to join *Mukti Bahini*. On or around 18 April I said good bye to them at the Shamibagh Bus Station in Dhaka for their voyage to an unknown destination and even uncertain destiny to India where the Resistance (*Mukti Bahini*) is rumored to being organized. Ulfat and Manzoor were the leaders, Ulfat being visibly and palpably the 'man in-charge'. He did not tell us where they were heading to; the only thing I knew that they were going to India (a huge country that surrounds the occupied Bangladesh on three sides), find the Resistance and join.

In contrast, the Pakistan-controlled radio was repeatedly telling us not to believe in rumors or

Confession of a Terrorist!
Chapter 1 Rendezvous

spread them. And then there were mushrooming of the graffiti calling for the people to take arms and fight, alongside the pre-existing ones from the recent past. The one that struck me most was a quote from *Netajee* Subhas Chandra Bose, my political hero from childhood "*Tomra amay rokto dao, ami tomay shadhinota debo*" (You give me blood and I shall get you independence/freedom)[4].

---

[4] Subhas Chandra Bose, adoringly called *Netajee* (term used for the beloved and revered leader) was one of the most prominent leaders of Indian independence movement. Working on the maxim that "the enemy of my enemy is my friend" he sought cooperation of Germany and Japan against British Empire during World War II. In January 1942 he started his regular broadcast from Radio Berlin giving great inspiration to the Indian masses yearning for freedom. He traveled to Soviet Union, Germany and Japan seeking their help in attacking the British in India. He formed the *Azad Hind Fauz* (Indian National Army) to put an end to the British colonial rule by force alongside the non-violent movement of Mahatma Gandhi; he led the Indian National Army in battle against the British in Imphal (Eastern-most part of India bordering Myanmar) and Myanmar (Burma). Imprisoned by the British authorities 11 times, he was as determined and patriotic as brilliant and has become a legend to all freedom-loving Indians (http://www.iloveindia.com/indian-heroes/subhash-chandra-bose.html). His famous motto was "You give me blood and I will get you independence/freedom."

Confession of a Terrorist!
Chapter 1 Rendezvous

The First Terrorist I Meet

It has been a while since Manzoor, Ulfat and Shelley had left and there was no news of them or from them. Not only the families were gravely concerned about their safety but this also did not help the conundrum: is there really a *Mukti Bahini* or not. So I waited and waited to get some definitive and credible information about the structure of *Mukti Bahini*, if there was one at all. That came in late May; one night between 20:00 – 21:00 Hrs. Ulfat suddenly appeared in Daliah's parents' house in Dhaka. Their house in Shamibagh being at the entrance of the city from the Comilla – Dhaka highway on the east (towards Agartala, Tripura in India) those days, it was a first safe haven; more logically so as Daliah's brother Shelley was his friend.

Ulfat's face became rugged, effusing bold determination and toughness even though he was physically quite slim, lanky just like me; his eyes were bulging and red in anger that looked even more fierce and menacing through the thick lenses of his eyeglasses. I could almost feel his blood boiling. I have only heard and read about volcanic eruptions; he seemed like one ready to blow up. For a brief moment he frightened me. Daliah's mother was

Confession of a Terrorist!
Chapter 1   Rendezvous

very nationalistic and quite a gutsy person; she too was taken aback. Sensing that, Ulfat forced a smile that was as obvious to him as to me and the rest of the people in presence. I was not just afraid *of* him, instantly I also became afraid *for* him, for he acquired the typical profile of a terrorist; if he would be seen by Pakistani military personnel or their spies or collaborating traitors, he would be instantly recognized and apprehended. He had a sack containing several hand grenades and a pistol. I guess he knew that he could be caught, and that's why he had the pistol and the hand-grenades with him; he was not going to give in that easily. And that would have been suicidal. He came back to do some "operations" in Dhaka – to the Pakistani's and all other illegal occupiers and forces "terrorist action." Now I saw a real *Mukti Bahini* - seeing is believing; it is rumor no more.

He told me that Capt. Dr. Akhtar Ahmed who was a year senior to me in Dhaka Medical College was in charge of organizing the medical care for our wounded Freedom Fighters; and that they needed physicians badly. That's it! I expressed my determination to offer my humble services to my motherland during the time of its need.

Confession of a Terrorist!
Chapter 1   Rendezvous

Ulfat had left his hand-grenades with Daliah's mother for safekeeping; she wrapped them in some clothes and carefully placed them on the floor of the bedroom as if the clothes were for laundry. This as you can guess was done to avoid being detected in the event the spies were following Ulfat and the Pakistan military would come to search the premises. Like the Israeli military, the Pakistani military (the only two countries in modern history to be carved out solely on the basis of religion) was practicing the barbaric but effective doctrine of collective punishment; if they would discover the hand-grenades, Daliah and her family members irrespective of age, sex, physical or medical condition would be tortured and killed and their house demolished as a warning to others. Fortunately that did not happen that night.

The next day Ulfat came back with his one and one-half year old nephew. The nephew in his arms and grenades in his nephew's diaper bag he went to the Court House in the old town in a rickshaw to explode them to announce to the demoralized Dhaka population that yes, there is a *Mukti Bahini*. Why only the Dhaka population? Only those people who have heard or seen the explosion would believe it and will be telling it to others; so the news would spread by 'word of mouth' like wildfire since the

Confession of a Terrorist!
Chapter 1   Rendezvous

regular news channels such as radio, television and newspapers were controlled by the Pakistani Military who would do everything to suppress this terrific reportage. The clandestine Radio Bangladesh (*Sadheen Bānglā Betar Kendro*) would announce it too, albeit a bit later as they have to be informed by reliable sources through underground channels. Ulfat was careful enough to explode them in a relatively clear area in an otherwise densely populated city especially the Court House area; no one was reported hurt. Yes, he had terrorized some people, yet we all loved it! The people now know that there is indeed a Resistance and that skyrocketed our morale.

I was a Final year MBBS student in Dhaka Medical College of the University of Dhaka who had passed his ECFMG[5] examination to come to USA as a physician the year before and was communicating with hospitals in USA. So even though I had not received my MBBS degree, I had the necessary

---

[5] MBBS is a medical degree that stands for Bachelor of Medicine and Bachelor of Surgery; ECFMG is Educational Council for Foreign Medical Graduates, a world-wide testing to recruit medical doctors for United States. The qualified physicians are then at par with the medical graduates of the United States of America and hence eligible for employment and further training in USA.

Confession of a Terrorist!
Chapter 1   Rendezvous

education, more or less as a medical doctor. My classmates Mohammed Abdul Hafiz and A. Q. M. Mahmood (alias Farooq, aka Farooq Mahmood), and I had deeper interest in learning emergency care; so we were working in the Emergency Room (ER) of Dhaka Medical College Hospital especially late at night, even before our curriculum required us to do. Besides, it was a convenient place to hang out to see interesting cases, out of the ordinary people, reactions of patients' friends and family etc. Three of the ER physicians, Drs. Adiluzzaman, Shamsul Haque and Hassan were especially interested in teaching us; they also appreciated the extra help during rush hours and our company in the wee hours of morning when it was quieter. This allowed us to gain much hands-on experience in emergency management that we would not otherwise have. Dr. Hassan took a particular interest and liking for us. He was a great teacher, even better than some of our professors; the best; he would let us handle complicated cases, of course under his supervision yet giving us as much independence as needed for our training; he would then reward our effort by treating us to *Hajji Shaheb's* famous chicken biriyani from the old town around 02:00 Hrs. when the ER was usually quiet. One of the things

Confession of a Terrorist!
Chapter 1   Rendezvous

Hassan *vai* [6](*vai* means brother, an affectionate but respectful salutation used to address or refer to superiors or upper-classmen) used to tell us about pediatric patients is that "you have to give some tranquilizers to the children's mothers before you start treating the children!"

After 25 March, Hafiz a student political think-tank with a leftist party but not too active in any organization that I knew of, had left for his hometown Magura. Mahmood being active in leftist political movement was keeping a low profile to avoid the indiscriminate harassment and torture by Pakistan army as his neighborhood was specifically targeted for intense search and destroy missions. During

---

[6] In Bānglā as in many other languages and cultures, elders are addressed with respect. Strange as it may read, inexplicably the Moslem elders are referred to as *vai* and Hindus as *Dada* (to be specific *-da* is added to the name e.g. Shonkor *da*) perhaps to make the communal distinction! As though absurdity has no limit, likewise elder brother's wife is referred to as *vabi* if Moslem and *Bou Dee* if Hindu. While mother's brothers are called *Mama* with no communal distinction[!], mother's sisters are called *Mashi* for Hindus and *Khala Amma* for Moslems; father's brothers are *Jetha* or *Jethu* (elder) or *Kaka* or *Kaku* (younger) for both Moslems and Hindus, some Moslem Bengalis especially in big cities of late prefer to call them all *ChaCha* without age distinctions. Sadly that's how strongly religion shuts off our brain cells from thinking rationally. Anyway, friends of parents are also addressed with respect as if they are their brothers or sisters using the same ludicrous format.

Confession of a Terrorist!
Chapter 1   Rendezvous

these days I therefore had the sole attention of my mentors gaining good and exclusive training in handling casualties; besides, many other medical students fearing for their life had left the hostels or dormitories to go to their homes or any other safe place, if there was one. From the day I told Ulfat about my desire to join *Mukti Bahini*, I redoubled my efforts virtually living in the ER; the fact that my parents were not in Dhaka was also very helpful. Of course, no one besides Ulfat knew anything about my plan, not even the dearest of my friends; especially them; for if by any chance the Pakistani military would want to find out about me they would be torturing my friends for information and perhaps eventually killing them. Alternatively, if they would be interrogated, my plans would be exposed following *their* torture.

Two days prior to my departure for Agartala in India, as usual late one night I was volunteering in the ER when Dr. Ashik walked in. Dr. Ashik used to be a leftist student leader belonging to EPSU (East Pakistan Students' Union) several years senior to us. He was popular and I was rather fond of him, till that night that is. He started to admonish me as to what was I doing in Dhaka and why have I not joined *Mukti Bahini*. "Aren't you being a hypocrite?" I replied; "as a leader you are the one who

Confession of a Terrorist!
Chapter 1   Rendezvous

should have gone and showed us the way." He was taken aback by my straight-talking answer as that is not my normal polite self; I have already transformed, hardened-up; I only have the Pakistani goons to thank for that! Ironically he had no clue that I would be gone in less than 48 hours! I could have told him about my planned departure, a) you could not trust anyone those days and b) I wanted him to be embarrassed for his behavior after he would find out that I had indeed joined the *Mukti Bahini*.

What about my parents? How would they view my leaving the country for the jungles in India and volunteering for the Liberation War? As if it was by a subconscious design, I had sent my parents and my siblings to our ancestral village in the district of Comilla, about 60 km south of Comilla town or ~25 km south of Laksham. After the famous speech by Sheikh Mujibur Rahman on 7th March 1971, I had strongly suspected that the way the events were unfolding, trouble was in the air; the Pakistani army will indiscriminately kill or hurt innocent civilians. Dad was a very determined and strong-willed person, but not too stubborn not to listen to his eldest son once in a while. I suppose that meant he had some respect for me too. Like most Muslims of his generation who wanted an

Confession of a Terrorist!
Chapter 1   Rendezvous

independent Pakistan, he had supported Muslim League during the days of Indian-Pakistani independence from the British, but he was never an active member. I, on the other hand though staunchly believed in Bengali nationalism, was not supporting any party; left leaning yes, positively viewed what socialism and communism had to offer to the masses, and liked what Chairman Mao Zedong wrote in his Red Book.

"Toom vee mosalmaan, haam vee mosalmaan"

Being born to Muslim parents, as a young man I too was indoctrinated to the religious teachings of Islam. Dad wanted me to recite the holy Koran every morning, which I most obediently did; Mom did not have any particular demands, she went along with Dad's wishes which seemed to fit her just fine. By the age of 14/15, I started to complain that I could not comprehend anything I was reciting from the Koran and to the best of my knowledge nor did they as none of us understood Arabic except being able to only read. What's the point? Then my dad made the worst mistake! He bought me a Koran with Bengali translation and now I understood what's in there for the first time! This was around the time when I was a second year medical student. One of the things that I found absurd was the Biblical story shared by Jews, Christians and Moslems alike and recounted in Koran whose impact is seen by the slaughtering of large domesticated animals (camel, cattle, lamb, goat etc) during the Muslim Eid festival. This is the story of Abraham presumably "asked by God" to sacrifice his son Ishmael to prove that Abraham loves God more than he loves his son, though the Jews believe that it was Isaac and not Ishmael.

Does it really matter which of his sons either Ishmael or Isaac that 'God wished him to sacrifice?' What kind of a 'compassionate' and 'merciful' God will ask that? And what kind of a father will try to comply with such a ghastly wish and commence to slaughter his own son? Yes, there are news stories of people conducting such disgusting acts for monetary or other interests; they are the lowly criminals and perhaps mentally unstable. How does that make Abraham a prophet revered by the three major monotheistic religions look like, a common criminal; someone who would murder his son for cattle, silver, gold, land etc.? Will my father be able to butcher me? Could I even think, much less be able to slay my son or daughter to prove my love of God or anyone? And worse, how could zillions of otherwise intelligent people since the days of Abraham actually believe in such ludicrous

Confession of a Terrorist!
Chapter 1   Rendezvous

story? Was Abraham schizophrenic? Could this have been cooked-up? True, these are hypothetical questions.

But there was another that was pertinent in real-life. Not wishing to offend anyone's feeling, suffice it to say that I also had serious problem in accepting another of the sayings that all non-believers [of Islam] would go to hell! I started to question: my childhood buddies Joydev and Profullo, my cousin Girendro and his mother my *Pishi* (father's sister) in my grandparents' village who would start making *shondesh* (Bengali candies made from dairy, molasses, coconut etc.) for me in advance when she knew that I was coming; my Dhaka Medical College friends Shushanto Bimal Dev, Horidas Biswas, Horipodo Ghosh, Bertin Guda, Boniface Costa (Barney), Michael Paris, Jeffrey Longu (from the Southeast African country of Malawi), my very dear sister-like Snighda *dee*, all "non-believers" of Islam, yet the most decent of human beings will go to hell? How can that be? If that's the case, I want to be there too, with them! Quite coincidentally the use of religion in politics strongly espoused by the Pakistan government to exploit the Bengalis with the infamous saying in Urdu *"Toom vee mosalmaan, haam vee mosalma-an"* (we're both Muslims, so… [I can exploit you!]) has also started to make me wonder.

Now the same regimes who preach Islamic brotherhood are unjustly denying the Bengalis, presumably their fellow 'Muslim brothers' their share of the power in government. What happened to the so called Islamic brotherhood? How in the name of your religion can one be unjust and cruel to one's "brother" and as the later events show massacre them and rape their sisters and mothers? How does religion serve me? The more I thought the more I was getting distant from my father who was a devout but far from being fanatic Moslem. Dad and I would argue back and forth about the value of religion and my agnostic views were not secret anymore. I could see that Dad did not endorse it, but he did not seem too uncomfortable about it either.

Dad was politically conscious but unlike a lot of his contemporaries not very vocal, let alone active. He would read the various newspapers and discuss, but I never saw him arguing strongly much less be in heated arguments as is common with Bengalis discussing politics. Heated may be an understatement; it is not uncommon for Bengalis, particularly

Confession of a Terrorist!
Chapter 1   Rendezvous

those from East Bengal to even shamefully engage in fist-fights.

On the subject of physical violence in political forums, it seems that the Bengalis have conveniently forgotten the barbaric killing of the Speaker of the Parliament of the East Bengal Legislative Assembly in the mid 1950's. During a Parliamentary session a brawl erupted; these supposedly civilized politicians started to beat each other; at one point the Speaker Mr. Shahed Ali Patwari from Chandpur in East Bengal (or East Pakistan) was hit with chair and/or flagpole and/or the metal stand of the microphone; he subsequently died of his injuries. The Bengalis of East Bengal have been quick to point to the Pakistanis or Indians or the British for their misery. Did any of these foreign powers teach the Bengali politicians to engage in a bar room-style fight and fatally beat the Speaker of the Parliament? This was during the days of short-lived *Jukto Front* (United Front) and Sheikh Mujibur Rahman (popularly called Sheikh Mujib) was in presence. Allegations of his involvement in the brawl and/or barbaric beating death of the Speaker remains disputed[7]. I was very young then, but I

---

[7] (http://priyo.com/blog/awami-league/26336.html posting of May 21 2009, 11:42 AM).The East Bengal Legislative Assembly was dominated by Muslim League, a pro-Pakistani political

Confession of a Terrorist!
Chapter 1   Rendezvous

distinctly recall Dad being very heartbroken and ashamed of this ghastly behavior by the politicians – the supposed leaders of our society. So, in my teenage period I too was not involved in politics or ardently supported anyone. To my utter surprise and a very pleasant one at that, Dad told me that he had voted for Awami League, not because he supported the party, but because that's how he could redress the injustice Pakistan government had done to us. Needless to say, I was ecstatic; I adored him even more.

I was most fortunate to have a wonderful relation with not only my mother, but also my father. My

---

party. In 1954 the various political parties espousing Bengali nationalistic ideals had united to form *Jukto Front* (*Jukto* meaning united) with a 21-point manifesto, two of the most important points being regional autonomy for East Bengal (East Pakistan), and Bengali as one of the State Languages. The politics became very muddy; the ruling West Pakistani minority did not want to relinquish their power to the majority Bengalis in East. During a session of the Legislative Assembly, a brawl broke up and in a most barbaric act, the Speaker of the House, who also happened to be a Bengali was killed! While Bengalis are always quick to point to the injustice by the Pakistanis and outsiders, I rarely see the mention, much less acknowledgments of such odious acts by Bengalis, intellectuals or otherwise. It is a shameful silence of the Bangladeshi intellectuals not to address who the murderer(s) of the Speaker was/were and not trying to bring them to justice. Ignoring it would not absolve the nation of its guilt.

Confession of a Terrorist!
Chapter 1   Rendezvous

relationship with Dad was very affectionate, loving, quite frank and unusually friendly compared to the standard in Bengali society those days. Dad took care of me since I was only 2+ years of age when my mom stayed back in the village for some time. He did everything a mother would do; he was "Mr. Mom" except that it was not a 'broken family' and it was in Dhaka in the early 1950's, specifically in Kurmitola near the old World War II airstrip that served as a supply point for British military in China, Indochina and the rest of South East Asia. We later moved to Tezgaon area in Dhaka. This had created a very deep bond between us, perhaps as strong if not stronger than that with my mother!

Dad was a phenomenal teacher. I did not start learning my alphabets the conventional way of 'A as an apple,' 'B as a boy' or *Ko, Kho, Goh,* etc. from traditional books. Dad would read the newspapers, those days the *Azad* or *The Observer* or *The Morning News* and teach me the alphabets from them. So, the first letter in English that I learnt was 'T' as in T̲he Observer or T̲he Morning News; likewise, the first letter in Bangla for me was *shorey-aa* from A̲*zad.* He knew that the news stories would make me fascinated enough to learn the basics! As if that was not enough, he would buy several books with increasing difficulties and

Confession of a Terrorist!
Chapter 1   Rendezvous

would mark each with Roman Numerals I, II, III, IV, up to IX or X. When I finished each one he would make me feel that I have accomplished a lot like graduating from one class (grade) to the next. Knowing that the punch line of a story is at the end, sometimes he would want me to read the last chapters so that I become interested in reading the rest of the book from the beginning. What a genius of a teacher; millions of thanks, Dad!!!

As to politics, Dad kept his opinions to himself; I suppose that he thought I was too young to be indoctrinated in politics. Dad made sure that I was not distracted from my goal – education; politics was not even tertiary. So my high school, college and medical college days were apolitical, but not unconcerned about our society or blasé.

The old Dhaka Airport in Tezgaon those days had only one runway that went north-south, most of the aircrafts landing would approach from the south and takeoff to the north. Our house in Tezgaon was about 3 km south of the south-end of the runway exactly on the flight path of the landing airplanes; they were flying barely 100 m over our house; the tallest and the first beacon was less than 20 m away. Usually most of the planes would be landing during the days and early evening; so the noise though

Confession of a Terrorist!
Chapter 1   Rendezvous

annoying was not unbearable. However, after 7th March, we could hear and see large planes landing every hour if not every half-an-hour after midnight. These planes sounded and looked different from the propeller driven Dutch Fokker aircrafts that were flying domestic routes or the British-made Vickers Viscount 815 turbo-prop or rear-mounted three-engine Trident and US-built four-engine Boeing 707 jets flying twice or thrice a day to and from Karachi and Lahore in West Pakistan; they were huge; in the dark of the night we could not see the details of the outside; but definitely these were not PIA (Pakistan Air Lines), rather unmarked and dark – the military C-130 transport planes we thought. And they were flying all night; but none after dawn! That was very suspicious. So, when the rumor was spreading that the Pakistan Government was sending troops to the East, I was convinced; you did not have to be genius to figure out what was going on.

Anticipating serious trouble ahead, when I told my father to go to the village with the rest of our family, he listened and left with my mother and my siblings for the village the following week (around 15-16 March). His younger brother was more stubborn than him and did not leave till the Pakistan army started to commit its carnage in his neighborhood.

Confession of a Terrorist!
Chapter 1   **Rendezvous**

Unfortunately, he paid the price; he was badly beaten on his way to the village. I never found out the reasons, perhaps as stubborn as he was, he must not have followed the orders when he encountered the omnipresent Pakistani military, or perhaps he became belligerent. Be that as it may, my parents, siblings, uncle and cousin were all in the village. So there was no drama or tearful and fearful goodbye for me; and nobody to hold me back.

My classmate Sabita Mondol's husband (Shonkor *da*) and her in-laws had fled to India for fear of their lives as they were Hindus and the Pakistani military was specifically targeting the Hindu population. Her father-in-law, a very respected and reputed judge in Comilla had arranged for her to join them across the border. Daliah's mother didn't think it was safe for Daliah to stay in Dhaka especially that one of Daliah's brothers - Shelley had presumably joined the *Mukti Bahini*; that alone makes the family vulnerable to persecution by the Pakistani goons.

Zeenat Yasmin was the top student in our class and I had made it my mission to dethrone her; so the two of us had this academic rivalry. Notwithstanding that, we had a very cordial and friendly relationship; her brother was also my classmate in Notre Dame College in Dhaka. Zeenat started to date an

Confession of a Terrorist!
Chapter 1　　　　　Rendezvous

upper classman and was very much in love. Being contented in her relationship and in bliss, she felt duty bound to help her friends! Zeenat started to act like a matchmaker and asked me if there was someone I liked.

Daliah entered Dhaka Medical College in mid-1967, two years after me. At 160 cm and 45 kg she was petite and slim; she had a distinct gait, walked straight with confidence yet style – she would stand out amongst all the rest of the girls, except her close friend and constant companion Shobnam, who according to most people was prettier. Daliah would wear the bell-bottom pants, fashionable at the time with colorful *kameez* (tops) up to her mid-thigh. Her face was oblong, forehead prominent with dark hair up to her shoulder and a pleasant smile. With a small nose and somewhat flat bridge she looked a bit Thai [a few people actually told her that] and effused intelligence. Sometimes she would be wearing a *sari* that would be stylishly wrapped around her waist and hip, rather snugly to look sexy in contrast to most women who wear it a bit loosely. She would place pleats and safety-pins or other contraptions to accentuate her otherwise modest curves; a distinctive way of wearing the *sari* that I had not seen too many women doing it, young or otherwise. There was a touch of elegance. With

Confession of a Terrorist!
Chapter 1   Rendezvous

trousers she would wear moderately high-heels; with *sari* matching sandals and blouses showing off her midriff. She knew how to make the best of her modest assets!

Daliah was not just pretty; she was one of the top students in her class. Intelligent people had always attracted me more than just the pretty ones, but Daliah had the lethal combination of both and more: she was cultured too. Daliah had learnt Bengali and Indian classical and folkdances at BAFA (Bulbul Academy of Fine Arts) and performed several shows on Dhaka Television. Thus, she was somewhat of a celebrity particularly amongst the youth, a television personality. In February the previous year (1970), I had expressed my liking for Daliah to Zeenat. She arranged for us to meet in a Chinese restaurant for lunch on the 14th [Valentine's Day, except that in those days it was not commercialized as it is now]. Thanks to Zeenat, it was the beginning of our courtship; on second thought, was it Zeenat's ingenious act of trying to get rid of her academic competition?!

Confession of a Terrorist!
Chapter 1   Rendezvous

Interlope

On 27 June 1971, the three of us (Sabita, Daliah and I) met our guide who was sent by Capt. Dr. Akhtar Ahmed, in Shamibagh at around 08:00 in the morning in Daliah's parent's house, a time chosen to appear that we are "normal" citizens going on to our "normal" business not to arouse suspicion by the omnipresent Pakistan army and their *Razakar*, *Al Bodor* and *Al Shams* stooges[8]. Our

---

[8] The Pakistan military had recruited pro-Pakistani Bengalis, mostly members of Islamic parties and Urdu-speaking-Moslem refugees from the Indian state of Bihar (hence called Bihari) to work as spies and in other capacities against the Bengali nationalist – they were called *Razakars*. Though we had welcomed the Bihari refugees with open-arms, they on the other hand did not make any effort to integrate with the host Bāngālis. They spoke only Urdu; made no effort to speak Bānglā and expected Bāngālis to speak their language - Urdu! Their allegiance was to the Urdu-speaking Pakistani rulers than their Bengali hosts. As such they considered themselves superior to the local Bengalis! [Strangely, the Bihari Muslim immigrants were not the only ones; even many Bengali Muslim refugees from West Bengal (WB) had this supercilious attitude. Daliah's mother, who hailed from Murshidabad WB, harbored the same condescension towards us – the host population, and this is *no* 'Mother-in-law joke'!] The *Razakars* were instrumental in identifying the members of the various Resistance movements, politicians, leaders, intellectuals etc. On many occasion they themselves had carried on the assassinations and torture. So that there is no misunderstanding, the overwhelming majority of the *Razakars* were however Bengali traitors who harbored religious fanaticism. The feared members of *Al Bodor*

Confession of a Terrorist!
Chapter 1   Rendezvous

intrepid guide knew all the usual military checkpoints along the way to Sonamura in the Indian state of Tripura (commonly referred to as Agartala, its capital) as he has done this a few times before, for there were military checkpoints throughout the land. To avoid those, we took a bus from Jatrabari in Dhaka to the east towards Daudkandi; but we got off about a kilometer before crossing the River Gomoti on the west bank because the Pakistan Army had a checkpoint on both the east and west banks. There was no bridge on the Rivers Gomoti or Meghna those days; one had to get on ferries to cross the rivers. Our boat dropped us off on the Daudkandi-Comilla highway near Chandina, again past any possible checkpoints. From Chandina we took two baby-taxis (auto-rickshaw) towards the city of Comilla[9]. Traveling east from Dhaka, Comilla military Cantonment is before the city; the Cantonment has been one of the five major sites of mass-killings in that district. Logically, it would be suicidal to

---

and *Al Shams* militia were carrying arms in the open, were more dangerous and they carried out the assassinations *ad libitum*.

[9] The district of Comilla came under the rule of the British East India Company the front of the British Colonialism in 1765; in 1790 it was established as Tripura District with the government headquarter in the town of Comilla – now a city. In 1960 the district was renamed to Comilla to distinguish it from the adjacent State of Tripura, India.

Confession of a Terrorist!
Chapter 1   Rendezvous

walk into the sharks' mouth; thus, a few kilometers short of the Cantonment we got off the baby-taxi and took two rickshaws on a dirt road to cross the Indian border. It took us about 10 hours to travel about 85-90 km; our modes of transportation varied from the slow-moving rickshaw to even slower moving boats, and baby-taxis to bus.

Rickshaws Riding on Passengers!

It was around 18:00 Hrs. and was getting dark, especially as it started to rain heavily. After we rode the rickshaws for a few minutes (hardly 200-300 m) the rickshaw drivers got off their seat and started to pull; the mud in the road made it impossible for the rickshaw drivers to paddle, the rickshaws had to be pulled. Since Sabita was leaving her motherland as a refugee, with the horror that she may never come back, she took all her belongings, or as much as she could, and those of her husband, Shankar *da*. Thus her suitcases took all of the space in both rickshaws; Daliah was sitting in one and Sabita in the other. The malnourished rickety rickshaw drivers were at a lost. Our guide was a trained Freedom Fighter and was strong, so he pushed the rickshaw with Sabita and one-half of her suitcases in it while the driver was pulling. I though not much stronger than the rickshaw-driver,

Confession of a Terrorist!
Chapter 1   Rendezvous

was doing the same with the rickshaw carrying Daliah and rest of Sabita's luggage. We did this for about 3-4 km till we came within a couple of hundred meters from the Level Crossing (railroad-crossing) on Comilla-Akhaura railroad; we could see that the railroad was at a higher level, about a meter higher than the dirt road which is deeply muddy by now.

Our route from Dhaka to Sonamura was along Highway N1 except while crossing River Gomoti by boat with a detour, and by rickshaw and by foot on dirt road from near the intersection of N1 and N102; Agartala is directly to the north of Sonamura (From Google Maps)

Railroad crossings in the erstwhile East Pakistan and now in Bangladesh are called Level Crossings which is a misnomer here. As in most railroad-

Confession of a Terrorist!
Chapter 1   Rendezvous

crossings for dirt-roads in Bangladesh, the train tracks were much higher than the muddy road and the rail-tracks at the crossing is far from being at the same level as the intersecting road surface, making it difficult to go across especially for rickshaws with big but very narrow frail wheels. This is not a place to waste any moment; time is critical, a second's delay may make the difference between life and death. The Pakistan army knows that the border is porous here; this is a route frequented by the Freedom Fighters to travel between India and the occupied Bangladesh and thus they patrol the railroad. They use a shuttle railway-wagon fitted with machine guns to go back and forth. The stepmotherly discrimination by the Pakistan Central Government against the Bengalis and the erstwhile East Pakistan had a paradoxical benefit; since this railroad was a single-track line it meant that they could not keep it under surveillance all the time as the regularly scheduled trains would be competing for the only track! Whenever I was distraught with some problems, my mother would say "look at the bright side son." "How can there be a bright side to this, Ma?" A pillar of strength, she would then recount a funny story to show me the positive side of an otherwise dismal picture. There is a silver lining on every dark cloud.

Confession of a Terrorist!
Chapter 1   Rendezvous

The rickshaw-drivers informed our guide about the schedule when the Pakistan army patrol would pass through our crossing and we timed the crossing accordingly. To be sure, our guide reconfirmed from the locals he was familiar with and trust, that the military patrol had just gone north and this is our only chance for safe crossing. Up until now we had been pushing the rickshaws in ankle-deep if not deeper mud in a relatively slow pace. But now we will have to run, run for our lives! I was about 58 kg and 178 cm; but I don't know how, all of a sudden I became a very strong man – almost a superman for a moment; I lifted the rickshaw with Daliah in it (we did not want the girls to get off as too many figures running and crossing could arouse the suspicion of the patrolling army) and half of Sobita's suitcases and ran for the next couple of hundred meters and at the railroad crossing pushed it across the rail-tracks on the other side while lifting it up about 20 cm or so. Inasmuch as the heavy rainfall caused enormous hardship on my poor body, it was a great blessing in disguise; the visibility was so poor that the Pakistan army shuttle wagon a few hundred meters away did not detect us. And that apparently was the last area on which the Pakistan army had control over.

Confession of a Terrorist!
Chapter 1   Rendezvous

Hoorah! Being on cloud nine and with this miraculous burst of energy and strength, we ran all the while pushing the rickshaws till we came to a bazaar (I believe it was either Baraipur or near it) about a kilometer or so away, close to the Indian border in the no-man's land. Here we let the rickshaws go. It was around 20:00 Hrs. and we barely travelled 5 km or so in 2 hours. I should have been dead tired, but I wasn't! Theoretically I had learnt in the medical college about how and when adrenaline kicks in during fright, but never seen an example of it. Surprisingly this time I learnt and felt about what adrenaline can do the first hand. That our destination - Sonamura would be 3-4 km from there was also a great motivational element.

Having come to a place safe from Pakistan army after this entire arduous trip, we had the urge to respond to nature's call. For our guide and I, that was not a problem; but the ladies had to go too and we had to find some privacy for them! This bazaar was quite a seedy place full of smugglers, local touts, *Razakars* and other shady characters, and I became apprehensive about the safety of Sabita and Daliah. But our guide assured me, and I saw that he was rather well known there; he had been a frequent interloper!

Confession of a Terrorist!
Chapter 1   Rendezvous

After we all had some time to breathe easily, we had some snacks, but wanted to go to a real safe-haven in India and not in a smugglers' den which is still within [the then] East Pakistan; retrospectively, it seems that we simply did not want to be in "Pakistan" anymore. So around 21:30 or 22:00 Hrs. we started again. We walked a short distance past some pyramidal concrete pillars demarcating the border between India and Pakistan; few hundred meters beyond which was a paved road! What a contrast in rural development between India and the then East Pakistan?! On one side of the border (still East Pakistan) we had to struggle through several kilometers of muddy road whereas on the Indian side there was a paved road right from the border!

I have seen this during my weeklong visit to Punjab and North-West Frontier Province of West Pakistan in 1968. As a student delegate I was part of 25-30 students from the then East Pakistan who were chosen presumably on the basis of merit to go to West Pakistan to promote "understanding" and "bonding" between the two parts of Pakistan. The project certainly was successful in my understanding of the great injustice the Pakistan government had been doing to us the Bengalis. Thanks to the project, I saw firsthand the enormous disparity in

Confession of a Terrorist!
Chapter 1   Rendezvous

development between the two parts of a supposedly one-country. There were paved roads connecting the remotest villages and electricity in Punjab, back in 1968. And here in India, they have the same; alas, my poor motherland has been so neglected.

We hired two rickshaws to travel a few more kilometers to Sonamura. The feeling of safety and the smoothness of riding the rickshaw on a paved road in contrast to the rickshaws riding on us and the other hardship that we have been going through for the past 14+ hours was making me drowsy; the exhaustion was rapidly spreading from my feet through the calf muscles and thighs to my entire body and finally my neck muscles and eyes; I could barely keep my eyelids open.

The First Supper

We arrived in Sonamura, a small border town that had a *daak bungalow* (Rest-House) for the Forest Department where Capt. Dr. Akhtar Ahmed had setup his "treatment facility" on the western edge of town, conveniently closest to the border. There was a paramedical person Subedar Mannan, a couple of lower-ranking enlisted men, Capt. Akh-

Confession of a Terrorist!
Chapter 1   Rendezvous

tar's batman[10] Taher, and Sabita's father-in-law the Honorable judge Rabindranath Biswas and his wife, and a journalist Shahadat *vai*. There were also two sisters, University of Dhaka students Sayeeda Kamal (Tulu) and Sultana Kamal (Lulu) who had arrived a couple of weeks prior; they were well known through their famous poet mother Begum Sufia Kamal. Then there were Bahar and Jamal the Freedom Fighters duo from Comilla who had the combination of being witty, courageous, hilariously funny with their local accents and extreme innovativeness. They were most famous for daringly hijacking a Mazda pick-up van fully loaded with all the medicine and medical supplies that it could hold along with a driver, from Comilla (Chouddogram Rural Health Center, I believe); because Capt. Dr. Akhtar told them that he did not have any medicine or medical supplies!

---

[10] Batman is an enlisted person assigned to an Officer to do all his chores, but also his body guard – ready to give his life for the Officer. Historically Subedar (a junior commissioned officer or JCO) is ranked below a British commissioned officer and above a non-commissioned officer, but was otherwise equivalent to Lieutenant in British military. It was introduced by the British colonials to facilitate communication with the native troops. As such the Subedars were required to be fluent in English. Until 1866 this was the highest rank an Indian could achieve in the Armies of British India. A Subedar's authority was confined to Indian troops; he could not command British troops [of course]!
http://en.wikipedia.org/wiki/Subedar

Confession of a Terrorist!
Chapter 1   Rendezvous

By the time we arrived at the *daak bungalow* it was around 23:00 Hrs. Being drenched in rain and the sweat from the fear of life and pushing and lifting the rickshaw and walking through mud, I could not wait to take a shower under the tube-well (inexpensive wells made of steel or lately polyvinyl chloride pipes with a cast-iron hand-pump mounted on top) before eating the meal that was offered to us. The meal was simple: rice with *daal* (lentils) and some sautéed vegetable (*labra*). We were the only ones eating as everyone else had already had their supper earlier, but they were sitting beside us, excitedly wanting to hear about our trip and the news from home. As I started to chew the first bite, I felt some stones (*kakar*)[11] in the rice; I stopped chewing for a moment and saw Capt. Dr. Akhtar looking at me. His look was very telling: eat it, that's the best you are going to get! I continued eating but suppressing my uneasiness in chewing the *kakar* every other or every third bite.

After the supper, Capt. Dr. Akhtar wanted to know what my intentions and plans were. He has seen many of us passing through Sonamura only to go

---

[11] Unscrupulous businessmen adulterate various commodities to increase their bulk or weight for bigger profit and rice being a staple for Bengalis is a common target which is commingled with stone chips.

Confession of a Terrorist!
Chapter 1   Rendezvous

to Kolkata and.... I had told him that I wanted to serve my motherland the best way I can – providing medical care. He was pleasantly surprised, even more so when he came to know that I already had passed my ECFMG to go to USA.

As I mentioned before, Capt. Dr. Akhtar Ahmed was a year senior to me in Dhaka Medical College.

Capt. Dr. Akhtar Ahmed at Saldanadi railway station after its liberation in early November 1971

Not too long after graduation, he had joined the East Bengal Regiment of Pakistan Army as a regimental medical officer (RMO). In the medical college, he enjoyed the reputation of being a "tough-

Confession of a Terrorist!
Chapter 1   Rendezvous

guy." As if to project that tough-guy image in here too he was sporting long bushy moustache; he has also grown long hair and he had this rugged face (see above picture) that was different from what I remember from his Medical College days. But he was clean-shaven. I did not think that this "tough guy" would remember me, but to my pleasant surprise he did, or was being polite to do so. So, we started discussing; he was telling me how he was part of the Company[12] (a unit of soldiers) commanded by Maj. Shafat Jamil had revolted in Brahmanbaria, birthplace of the legendary hero of Indian independence - Aviram[13], proceeded north to Sylhet, met up with Majors Khaled Mosharraf, Zia,

---

[12] A Company is a military unit usually consisting of 75-200 soldiers and commanded by a Major - the Commanding Officer (CO) or Officer Commanding (OC), as in the British army, with a Captain or a senior Lieutenant as second in command (2i/c). Most Companies are formed of three to five platoons. Several Companies are grouped to form a Battalion and several Battalions form a Regiment. The Companies are designated as A, B, C, D, E and sometimes the head-quarter Company. A is referred to as Alpha, B: Bravo, C: Charlie, D: Delta, E: Echo which are phonetically convenient to reduce confusion.

[13] Ullaskar Dutta (or Datta) also known as Aviram was born in the Village of Kalikaccha in Brahmanbaria. He manufactured the bombs used by Khudiram Bose, Hem Chandra Das and other revolutionaries to assassinate the British colonial officers. He was exiled to the Andaman by the occupying British.

Confession of a Terrorist!
Chapter 1   Rendezvous

Shafiullah, Colonel Osmani and high-ranking Indian military and B̲order S̲ecurity F̲orce (BSF) officers. It was exciting as I have only heard their names in the clandestine radio news reports of *Shadheen Bānglā Betar* (Radio Free Bānglā); now to hear from someone who has actually seen and met them was thrilling, and reassuring. Then he told me how they retreated to India, set up his "field ambulance" a US television series MASH-type medical unit (but closer to the line of fire than M*A*S*H) which is almost always at the risk of being hit by bullets and bombs, not too far from here. I could listen to these hair-raising accounts of his bravery, dedication and patriotism not just that night all-night, but for days in a row. But behind that macho "tough-guy" war hero image was a very kind man with tender heart and subdued ego that his sweet smile gave away. He knew I needed rest, so he essentially ordered me to get some sleep; that was around 03:00 Hrs. a time I normally wake up! I was not [and still am not] used to being ordered around; but it was a very pleasant feeling – one that was mixed with concern for my wellbeing and affection towards a younger brother.

Confession of a Terrorist!
Chapter 1   Rendezvous

Slumber Party

The bungalow was situated at the extreme western end of the town, next to the River Gomoti on the south. While the main town of Sonamura was about 3-4 km from the border, the bungalow was only about 2 km or less away from the Pakistan army bunkers across the border, on the opposite side of River Gomoti. Apparently, the area around the bungalow or Rest-House used to be a forest of *shaal* (tall trees that are used for timber) before it was inhabited. Naturally, the Rest-House was built of wood (*shaal kaath*). While the mighty river Gomoti is quite wide in the west in Daudkandi area, nearly 2 km in width, in here closer to its origin it was only a couple of hundred meters or less in breadth. The River Gomoti can be devastating in the rainy season causing severe flood along its route, and there are embankments on either side to protect the inhabitants. The Rest-House, perhaps due to this perennial flooding and to avoid the attacks from wild-life, snakes etc. was built on stilts ~2 meters above the ground. It was facing south towards the River Gomoti and there was a staircase from the front porch to the embankment which was also a paved road. There were three rooms: as you walk up the stairs you directly face the sitting room (living room). There were very few furniture,

Confession of a Terrorist!
Chapter 1   Rendezvous

certainly not enough for more than 2-3 people to sit; hence a lot of floor-space! There was one bedroom each on either side of the living room. Again, bedrooms with hardly any beds!

The Freedom Fighters get their training in the dense jungle of Melaghor, about 5-7 km northeast in the interior of Tripura State. Following completion of their training they cross the border to carry out commando operations (to terrorize the Pakistani military, cut-off their supply-line by blowing bridges and in the process, boost the morale of Bengalis) in their enemy-occupied motherland. The proximity of Sonamura to the border and the ease of communication with Melaghor make it a convenient entry/exit point. Notwithstanding the "tough-guy" image that Capt. Akhtar had in the medical college, he was revered by the young Freedom Fighters, especially those from Dhaka. Fondly and lovingly they called him "Doc." He and the presence of sisterly figures like Lulu, Tulu *et al* were added reasons for these teenage kids to stop by the bungalow before they slip across the border in the dead of night to avoid being caught or killed by the Pakistan army. Though they try their very best to hide their apprehension and project a macho image, it was no secret that they were going on to very dangerous missions; their return is not gua-

Confession of a Terrorist!
Chapter 1   Rendezvous

ranteed; they could get killed or worse caught, mercilessly tortured and then killed. The emotions were mixture of fear, pride, anxiety and anything else you can think of. Even joy may be; because these daring young patriots are going to hurt the Pakistan army.

So, the Rest-House bungalow was overcrowded to put it mildly as groups of Freedom Fighters would routinely spend a night, or a large part of the night as they pass through. Only one room had a bed that was quite appropriately used by the Hon. Judge Rabindranath Biswas and his wife. Of course there were no other beds, nor any bedsheets or pillows, and I did not expect any either; as a matter of fact I was expecting to be in tents in deep jungles; it was certainly a much upgraded accommodation in Sonamura 'Sheraton' at the riverfront! I prepared myself to sleep on the bare wooden floor which was quite uneven; the wooden planks were about 1-2 cm higher and lower to each other with 1-2 cm space between them. I took off my boots and used those as pillow and instantly fell asleep amongst 7-8 others.

CHAPTER 2

JUNGLE CAMP

After about three hours of sleep, my usual, I woke up around 06:00 Hrs. and could not wait to see the surroundings in daylight. Behind (to the north and east) of the Rest-House were some other tin-shed houses that had served as the office for the Forest Department and were later given to the *Mukti Bahini* for use as a Hospital in early May. This is where the patients were treated, and housed the meager medical supplies; this also housed the kitchen and living space for Subedar Mannan, Batman Taher, cooks and others. To the east there was an average sized pond approximately 40 x 60 meters that the local people used

Confession of a Terrorist!
Chapter 2   Jungle Camp

mostly to bathe and swim. We however used the tube-well water for shower.

Sonamura is a nice little town, a very neat and clean place. It is hilly – the hill is on the north and the mighty River Gomoti to the south with several of its serpentine bends. The local hospital, post office and the town is on the hill about a kilometer away from the Rest House. The people are extremely nice, friendly and not only willing but also anxious to help us. It seemed that though we all (the locals and us from East Bengal) are both Bengalis, they could immediately spot us as the newcomers from East Bengal! It must have been our rugged appearance, anger and determination in our face, our clothes. But they embraced us with open arms and smiling face as if they have just found their long-lost brothers; indeed, brothers we are, one Bengali nation, isn't it?

Sector 2 Head-Quarter

At or around 10:00 Hrs. Capt. Akhtar suggested that we go and visit the Head-Quarter in Melaghor, to which I excitedly said yes. I have heard about the *Mukti Bahini* and I wanted to see it all – 'seeing is believing'. It was a short 15-20 minutes ride on the Mazda pickup van that was hijacked from the

Confession of a Terrorist!
Chapter 2   Jungle Camp

erstwhile East Pakistan and then permanently stationed at the hospital. Gafoor, the driver who too was hijacked by Bahar and Jamal along with the van stayed on to serve the *Mukti Bahini*. Gafoor was an average Bengali man, about 165 cm, 50 kg, very soft spoken and polite. However, not unlike most drivers in East Pakistan, he was not the best; but was good enough and safe, more or less. Certainly he was the only driver; with Capt. Akhtar and me sitting next to him, he tried to drive very carefully; one could see he was nervous.

The Head-Quarter also served as the training camp for the Freedom Fighters who would be going into the Pakistan-occupied Bangladesh to commit 'acts of terrorism' and guerilla warfare. It was an impressive complex. There was a sentry-post at the entrance. The guard recognized Capt. Akhtar, gave a smart salute, and let us through. It was a dense jungle (*shaal bagan*). I had seen pictures of Vietcong guerillas fighting for *their* homeland in the jungles of Vietnam. But this is the real thing – not a picture, but picture-perfect. There must have been several thousand Freedom Fighters (it was estimated that there were a total of about 20,000 Freedom Fighters in this Sector that includes the Head-Quarter and the various Sub-Sectors), mostly young men in their teens, even boys. They wore pants and shirts

Confession of a Terrorist!
Chapter 2   Jungle Camp

or colorful *lungi* (a sarong or skirt-like) and shirts. For the summer heat and the humidity (this was the monsoon season) *lungi* and sandal was the preferred amongst those from the villages. The boys from the cities, especially from Dhaka would be wearing pants, but again mostly sandals (flip-flops) as footwear. Then there were some battle-tested regular military men who had fought on the side of Pakistan during India-Pakistan wars and now revolted along with their officers from the regular Pakistan military units or East Pakistan Rifles (EPR – a border-guard organization). Their battle-hardened faces showed all the features of anger, strong determination and defiance. They too were mostly casually dressed in *lungi*, shirt and sandals. The heat and humidity was so oppressive that some of the civilian support staff would be wearing *lungi* with only an undershirt and thongs. For practical reasons, I decided to preserve my boots clean for use as pillow and opted for the flip-flops instead.

The Freedom Fighters lived in barracks made mostly of bamboo and some timber; there were several of those barracks. The Commanding Officer Maj. Khaled Mosharraf was not there at the time we visited; he was touring the various Sub-Sectors. Capt. Akhtar introduced me to the Second-in-Command 2i/c Brigade Major Matin, Capt. Haider of Special Forces, and a few other officers. The Officers were all dressed in trousers and shirts, some in jeans and combat boots. It seemed that they preferred the safari shirts befitting their habitation in the dense jungles. Capt. Haider was specifically in charge of guerilla training; his trainees had [mostly] successfully carried out commando ("terrorist") operations against Pakistan military. An average Bengali in physical size, his face and demeanor was however very striking; he effused an aura of fearlessness along with cool head. I could sense that Capt. Akhtar was somewhat proudly introducing me to these regular military officers; perhaps because I too was from his profession, or because he looked at me like his younger brother (while I knew of him in Dhaka Medical College, I never met him before last night in Sonamura), or because unlike others of our profession, I was one of the few who did not move on to Kolkata but wanted to serve the *Mukti Bahini*, or all of the above.

Dhaka Medical College was a microcosm of the national politics. As 'birds of the same feather flock together' most students gravitate towards one student political party or another and they become close to each other, rarely if ever socializing with members of a different party. I, of course was one

Confession of a Terrorist!
Chapter 2   Jungle Camp

of the rare aberrations. Though I had left-leaning political views, I was not affiliated with any political parties; I had close friends across the parties and would hang out with them irrespective of their political viewpoints or affiliations. As to the contemporary politics of the time, all I cared about is liberation of my motherland. Prior to coming to India, to my utter dismay I had learnt during this rather brief period in our national catastrophe, that there is political infighting between various parties even in exile! So it was a breath of fresh air that the *Mukti Bahini* forces that I encountered here and as told by Capt. Akhtar, had no political affiliation or association; it was the Bangladesh Forces, loyal to the provisional government no matter which party was in power; Awami League happened to be the party that won the election and the legitimate political party that formed the government-in-exile. Of course, individual Freedom Fighters had their own political views and affiliations; however most who were trained here apparently were simple patriots without much political association if any; all they wanted was to fight the Pakistani military and liberate their homeland. There were other training camps specifically for those who identified themselves as members of Awami League or other parties, but not here at Melaghor. And that fit me perfectly!

Confession of a Terrorist!
Chapter 2   Jungle Camp

But my contentment was rudely interrupted rather abruptly. Capt. Akhtar of course wanted to proudly show me the fruit of his organizational labor. He is the person responsible for providing and administrating the medical support to all the Sub-Sectors and the Head-Quarter. So naturally he took me to the medical facility where I met one of my medical school-mate Mohammed Zubayer, 2 years junior to me (3rd year medical student). Zubayer was responsible for the medical care there along with Dr. Nazim who was a recent graduate from Mymensingh Medical College. It seemed that Zubayer was extremely popular amongst the Freedom Fighters. He took me to the side and within earshot of Capt. Akhtar was indoctrinating me to his politics – that of Awami League. He had wrongly assumed that I was a member of Awami League and he was fomenting divisive party politics. Being already sensitized to this malicious environment prior to leaving Dhaka, I without wasting a moment divulged to Capt. Akhtar what Zubayer was trying to convince me of, in his presence; having no defense, he was dumbfounded. Apparently Capt. Akhtar was aware of Zubayer's semi-subversive activities; it became transparent as to why he was giving away all the medicines, vitamins, anything to the Freedom Fighters in an overzealous manner, no matter whether

Confession of a Terrorist!
Chapter 2   Jungle Camp

they needed or not. No wonder he was popular! Through this line of action, he was trying to introduce party-politics amongst the non-political or apolitical Freedom Fighters. Capt. Akhtar instantly relieved him of his duty – an example of "zero tolerance" practiced by the *Mukti Bahini* as a general rule. I was more stunned than impressed; that, I did not expect and not instantaneously. But that's the way it was. Zubayer then quite appropriately joined the Indian military-run training camp for the Awami League Freedom Fighters in some other location.

Wow! What a first day in the life as a member of the *Mukti Bahini* and the day just started! I could not help but feel a bit guilty for getting Zubayer sacked; Capt. Akhtar reassured me that it was the right thing to do.

I was told by Capt. Akhtar that the food in the Officers' Mess in the Head-Quarter was better than in the hospital in Sonamura and strongly recommended that we have lunch there. In Sonamura, lunch is modest of flat bread (*chapatti*) and *daal* (lentils); rice with gravel-chips is served only at supper so that in the dim of light one is not likely to detect them visually and go to the next step – put in your mouth and chew; by the time you feel in your teeth, it's too late – swallow! Thus, he did not have to twist my arm for having a better lunch at the Head-Quarter. Like a camel storing water in its stomach for the hard days ahead, we ate as much as we could so that we could go easy on our supper of rice mixed with gravel chips that evening. After lunch we returned back to the Rest House in Sonamura.

General Yahiya's Speech

Not only is the Rest House a favorite stop area for the outgoing Freedom Fighters infiltrating the occupied Bangladesh and incoming new potential recruits and any other guests, it was also a popular hangout place amongst the various Sub-Sector commanders and their companions, thanks to the popularity of Capt. Akhtar. Another factor was that in order to go to some of the southern Sub-Sectors such as Dhonpur and Nirvoypur, one has to cross the River Gomoti by a ferry and the ferry *ghat* (boarding ramp/dock/area) was only meters away from the Rest House. Later that afternoon I had a very pleasant surprise – another lanky, tall but rugged-looking *Mukti Bahini* Officer sporting a moustache parked his jeep with a bit of a commotion outside the Rest House; he was blaring his

Confession of a Terrorist!
Chapter 2   Jungle Camp

horn and yelling at someone; obviously he was looking for attention, and attention he gets. Before Capt. Akhtar could introduce me to him by saying this is Captain Fazlul Kabir, I immediately recognized him as my old classmate from Notre Dame College (1963-1965) in Dhaka and so did he: Oh what a wonderful surprise it was!

For strategic planning and tactical purposes the various parts of occupied Bangladesh were designated into different sectors, Comilla/Agartala area being Sector 2; the Sectors were then divided into several Sub-Sectors. My old classmate Fazlul Kabir (now retired as a Major General) was the Sub-Sector commander of Dhonpur which along with Nirvoypur Sub-Sector (commanded by Late Capt. Mahboob) was south of Sonamura. Thus they had to cross the River Gomoti and the Rest-House Hospital was a convenient stop.

I remember Capt. Kabir from our Notre Dame College-days as a fun-loving and adventurous man. No matter how hard he tried to look truculent by sporting a mustache and menacingly popping his eyes wide open to his subordinates, he could barely hide his soft heart with his characteristic smile and a laugh – with sounds emanating deep from his throat. Today is 28 June 1971 and General Yahiya

Confession of a Terrorist!
Chapter 2   Jungle Camp

the military ruler of Pakistan, is scheduled to address the "nation" on the radio in the evening I believe at 18:00 Hrs. I do not recall who had this idea, but I think it was Capt. Kabir who was at least one of them to propose that as a response to General Yahia's speech we shell the Pakistan Army position! As exciting as the idea was, I was ecstatic when Kabir invited me to see the action in the front! He invited the girls too. We started to walk west along the embankment towards the border and to a wooded area.

Capt. Kabir's men were already in the jungle with mortar and guns ready to fire. The mortar is positioned at an angle; the trajectory and the distance the mortar-shell travels depend on the angle at which it is firing. For accurate target-hit the angle has to be adjusted. So it is imperative that the gunner has input as to where the shells are landing and where the intended targets are. A man, I believe regular army personnel climbed up the tallest tree (observation post or OP) with his wireless communication to serve as lookout. At precisely the time General Yahiya began his speech, so was the barrage of mortar attack! The lookout was telling the gunners to adjust the mortars' angle, the intended targets – *Yahoo*! After making a couple of adjustments of the mortars' angles the lookout

Confession of a Terrorist!
Chapter 2   Jungle Camp

reported that the Pakistan army bunkers were hit and we jumped in excitement.

Based on prior experience and war tactics, Capt. Kabir felt that our reply to the General should be brief lest the Pakistan army spotted us, for they too can follow the trajectory of the incoming fire and locate the source and start shelling our position with much superior firepower. After several rounds of fire which lasted may be 4-5 minutes or less and served its purpose to demonstrate the Pakistanis that *Mukti Bahini* is alive and can give appropriate response, and to boost the morale of our countrymen trapped inside, that we are fighting for them, we hurriedly retreated to a safer location and eventually back to the hospital celebrating; we virtually danced all the way back to the Rest-House in ecstasy. Wow! The day I join the *Mukti Bahini* I get to see them in action; what a great fortune! What a day, and it isn't over yet!

Meeting the Hero

A few people became legendary during this short period of Resistance in the history of Bangladesh; first and foremost was Major Ziaur Rahman who gave life to the nation after the onslaught of 25th

Confession of a Terrorist!
Chapter 2   Jungle Camp

March, later on became the President of Bangladesh and then killed by his own people, just like the poem "The Patriot" by Robert Browning![1] Major

---

[1] http://www.readbookonline.net/readOnLine/2849/

The role of Major Ziaur Rahman on or after 25th March is not without controversy. Many believe that he not only remained loyal to the Pakistan regime to the end; but also appeared to have been indifferent to the Bengali cause. In Chittagong, a port city in southern Bangladesh, when Capt. Rafiqul Islam of EPR (the paramilitary border force - <u>E</u>ast <u>P</u>akistan <u>R</u>ifles), on his own, had started rounding up the Pakistani soldiers, apparently Major Zia tried to dissuade him. While Capt. Rafiqul Islam was boldly confronting Pakistani troop, Major Zia was on his way to the port to unload arms and ammunitions from M. V. Swat and bring them to the cantonment for the Pakistan Military! During this time Pakistani troops suddenly attacked the Bengali soldiers of the East Bengal Regimental Center around midnight; taken by surprise most of them were massacred in their bed including the Commanding Officer Col M. R. Chowdhury, all the while Major Zia was dutifully at work in the port supervising the unloading of the weapons from the ship, the very weapons that were going to be used against us! Only after he was warned by Capt. Khalikuzzaman, that his own life was in danger he jumped into action. Major Zia then decided to move out of the barracks with his troops and fled to Kalurghat across the river. After the local Freedom Fighters had already ceased the radio-station at Kalurghat, Maj. Zia arrived there with his troops, and went on the air as the '*Head of the Republic*' proclaiming it as the *Shadheen Bānglā Betar Kendro* or "Free Bangladesh Radio" and called on the people to fight the Pakistani military [I did not hear this first announcement]. However, the local civilian leaders dissuaded him from proclaiming himself as the '*Head of the Republic*' as that may be construed as a military coup; and in a second speech

Confession of a Terrorist!
Chapter 2 Jungle Camp

Khaled Mosharraf comes next; in his sector (Sector 2) he commanded enormous popularity and respect for his brilliant military planning and executions. He goes from Sub-Sector to Sub-Sector on a routine basis to go over the strategy, tactics and all the rest of the military operations stuff. Either by design or out of necessity he would stop by the Hospital in Sonamura (as mentioned earlier one has to cross the River Gomoti by ferry and the ferry *ghat* is near the Rest-House). It was a favorite hangout place for many. I don't recall whether it was the next day or the day after, he came to the Hospital. I have only heard about his good looks and his battle prowess, but this day I was introduced to him and so was Daliah as we were the latest additions to his forces.

Maj. Zia corrected himself and spoke on behalf of *Bongobondhu* Sheikh Mujibur Rahman, the Prime Minister-elect. It has been alleged that later on as President of the country (1976-1981) he helped rehabilitate individuals who were involved in the assassination of Sheikh Mujibur Rahman.

http://en.wikipedia.org/wiki/Ziaur_Rahman
http://en.wikipedia.org/wiki/Talk:Ziaur_Rahman

Confession of a Terrorist!
Chapter 2   Jungle Camp

Major Khaled Mosharraf, Sector Commander, Sector 2
Source: Google

At about 175 cm and 70 kg or so, in his mid-thirty's and movie-star-handsome, he had a very impressive presence. He wore olive-green trouser with olive-green safari-shirt, military combat boots; an automatic pistol in his holster was very conspicuous. He had a sharp nose and wide forehead; slightly receding frontal baldness with thinning hair made him look more like in his early forties, perhaps making him even more striking. He appeared more brainy than brawny. His dress, gait, and overall style and demeanor was as if borrowed

Confession of a Terrorist!
Chapter 2 Jungle Camp

from Hollywood Westerns; a John Wayne type of a character. He was not as talkative as the John Wayne character though, in that department he was less loquacious, more like a Clint Eastwood character. The sisters Lulu and Tulu had already met him as they arrived about 2 weeks before us; they were ogling. My beloved Daliah was in awe; she seemed to have been in the presence of a prince or a royalty. She was smiling incessantly, her voice was crackling with excitement, and titillated she was; her eyes were fixed on his face the entire time; the world could pass by and she couldn't bother.

Major Khaled Mosharraf did not talk much with me, just hello and welcome; but was discussing matters of military operations with Capt. Akhtar in a soft but firm and impassioned manner. At one point, it seemed that he was complaining about the politicians [nothing new there!] and higher commands including the Commander-in-Chief Colonel Osmani within our earshot.

Dr. Roy Choudhury

The next day Capt. Akhtar wanted me to go to Agartala with him. Thanks to the military government of General Ayub Khan, the dictator of Pakis-

Confession of a Terrorist!
Chapter 2   Jungle Camp

tan who in early 1968 had framed charges of sedition against Sheikh Mujibur Rahman and 34 other Bengali nationalist, the so called Agartala Conspiracy Case, the name of the town Agartala was quite well known to us. The defendants were charged with conspiring with India to destabilize Pakistan; the main conspiracy being supposed to have taken place in the town of Agartala, here in Tripura, India. The accused were jailed and one of them, an Air Force Sergeant Zahirul Haq was shot dead point-blank at the door of his jail cell by a Pakistani Habildar (a non-commissioned officer) while he was under trial! This dastardly act added fuel to the ongoing firestorm outside the jail house; the Bengali nation was not naive to accept this sham of a conspiracy and was doing mass protests, eventually resulting in the fall of General Ayub Khan's dictatorship, only to be replaced by another dictator - General Yahiya in 1969! In the process Sheikh Mujibur Rahman was catapulted from relative obscurity to national eminence. Needless to say, I was very, very curious to see what this famous Agartala looks like. Then there is this common saying "Agartala or Chokirtala" [contrasting the dismal ambiance under the bed or *Chokir-tala* versus the town of Agartala]. Is it as bad as *chokir-tala* or is it a magnificent town?

Confession of a Terrorist!
Chapter 2   Jungle Camp

On the way to Agartala we first passed Melaghor which I had already been two days prior. We traveled through the valley with hills and hillocks on either side. We passed Bishramgong and Bishalgorh; there were pineapple fields and jackfruit orchards interspersed with dense jungles of tall trees; occasional small settlements and bazaars also dotted the landscape. The roads are windy often with very sharp curves. Gafoor our driver was not an expert. Though I had been a motorcycle rider for 7-8 years by then, I never drove a car; but I was a bit apprehensive about Gaffor's skill as a driver. Capt. Akhtar too did not have much confidence in Gaffor's driving especially with the heavy trucks coming from the opposite direction. Compounding the fear was the ever presence of cows who had the right-of-way; in India as you know, cows are revered, hitting one would be suicidal; whereas drivers in East Pakistan, no thanks to two decades of undemocratic and military rule, have no respect for the right-of-way for human, let alone cows. As we approached Agartala, Capt. Akhtar took over the driving. Agartala is about 50 km from Sonamura, crow-flight would be less; but it took us nearly two hours to come, or so it seemed.

We first arrived at the Govind Ballabh (GB) Hospital named after an activist of independence of India

Confession of a Terrorist!
Chapter 2   Jungle Camp

Pandit Govind Ballabh Pant[2], who was honored with the title of *Bharat Ratno*; Pandit Pant had worked with both *Mahatma* Gandhi and *Netajee* Subhas Chandra Bose. He was also famous for championing the cause of Hindi as the national language or *rashtro bhasa* of India. Curiously Capt. Akhtar had ignored the main entrance and parked at the rear of the building. At the GB Hospital I was introduced to Dr. Roy Choudhury, a senior surgeon. A very polite, courteous and warm Dr. Roy Choudhury was like an elder brother (*Dada*) to Capt. Akhtar; instantaneously, he became one of mine too. When he heard that I just came from the Pakistan-occupied Bangladesh only a couple of days ago he affectionately put his hand on my shoulder. He did not have to say much, and he did not; but the touch said "*don't worry, we are here, everything will be fine and we'll take care of you my little brother.*" Indeed, he did; with my ECFMG qualification that makes me eligible to be a physician in USA (I had a copy of the certificate with me), he signed me up as a physician with the Indian Red Cross and arranged for a monthly salary I believe of about 250 Rupees. That was the first order of business followed by some small talks, "how is *Bou-Dee*"[3] etc. Then he walked us to the

---

[2] http://en.wikipedia.org/wiki/Govind_Ballabh_Pant
[3] *Bou Dee* means elder brother's wife

Confession of a Terrorist!
Chapter 2   Jungle Camp

medical store room and left me and Capt. Akhtar alone simply saying "go ahead." When we came to GB Hospital I was puzzled as to why Capt. Akhtar had parked our Mazda pick-up van in the rear of the hospital and not the front; I didn't ask him to find out why.

After Dr. Roy Choudhury (by now my *Dada* too) had left us in the medical store room closing the door behind him, there was no one else, only Capt. Akhtar and I. With a tone of immense hurry Capt. Akhtar told me to pick up any medicine that I deemed was necessary for our Hospital in Sonamura and stuff them in the pockets; in other words – steal! I hesitated for a moment; it was not something I had done before. But this is a different time; I understood instantly as to what he meant; a desperate situation calls for desperate action. Sensing my dithering Capt. Akhtar with a firm voice essentially ordered me to get on with it. We pocketed as much antibiotics as we could and hurried through the back door – surprise! The sky-blue Mazda pickup van was just outside; I got the answer as to why he had parked the car there! In essence, Dr. Roy Choudhury had set us up to steal whatever we needed; after all he could not formally give us any of those against the regulation forbidding assistance to *Mukti Bahini* by Red Cross

Confession of a Terrorist!
Chapter 2   Jungle Camp

affiliated Hospital. The low-level managers are the ones who have to 'go by the book' and he does not want to put them in a dilemma; I am sure they too wanted to extend their helping hand to us, but their hands are tied by regulations; *Dada's* was not; he could circumvent. As you can imagine, we could not have taken a whole lot of medicine in four of our pockets; better something than nothing.

That was not the end of Dr. Roy Choudhury's complicity. Capt. Akhtar, the driver Gafoor and I then went to his house; *Bou-Dee* had the lunch ready. It was sumptuous. By the time we finished lunch it was already getting dark; we had a lot to eat; just tells you how gracious their hospitality was. We then went to the Indian Border Security Forces Head-Quarter (91 BSF). Capt. Akhtar had to take care of some official business; perhaps as instructed by Maj. Khaled Mosharraf the day before. We spent the rest of the time in the Officers' Mess, dined there with the Indian paramilitary officers and slept in some of the spare accommodations rather comfortably, relatively speaking.

Confession of a Terrorist!
Chapter 2   Jungle Camp

My First Patient...

...was a Freedom Fighter from Nirvoypur Sub-Sector. He was a teenager, hardly 15 or 16, a very boyish innocent face which he was trying to give it a macho image by growing a few scraggly facial hair and nascent mustache. He was in pain, but that too he was doing his best to mask with a forced smile for me and perhaps more so for the girls. Though sisters Lulu and Tulu were liberal arts students at the University of Dhaka they had experience in tending to the needs of sick and wounded through their volunteer work following waves of devastating annual cyclones and tornados in Bangladesh. Capt. Akhtar used to be part of those Relief Teams going to the affected areas with medical and other help; of course, knowing him, he would not waste any time or opportunity to train them. Still, he gave them further training during the past 2 weeks they have been here. Daliah was a third-year student at the Dhaka Medical College, a period when medical students begin their clinical rotation in hospital words, outpatient clinics and the emergency room. So, she too had some experience in patient management. These young ladies were also pretty; which teenage boy would not project a macho image to impress them?

Confession of a Terrorist!
Chapter 2   Jungle Camp

The Freedom Fighter had taken a couple of shrapnel with wounds which ranged from 1-2 cm in maximum width, one in his left thigh and the other on his belly. My immediate concern was for the belly; thank goodness, fortunately it did not go through the layers of skin and fascia (the abdominal wall) into his belly cavity (abdominal cavity). I breathed a sigh of relief. Now is the task of taking the splinters out. Capt. Akhtar was not in Sonamura; with his [misplaced] confidence in me, he decided to go to his more important tasks of organizing the medical care in the various Sub-Sectors, procuring medical supplies etc. I asked Subedar Mannan, the medical assistant for a pair of gloves and some forceps (tweezers of various sizes and shapes and designs). He gave me a vacant look that said it all: there is none. This is another thing I learned very quickly here: how to read people's eyes; I learnt from Capt. Akhtar's look during the First Supper and now Subedar Mannan's. I washed my hands with soap, Mr. Mannan poured some rectified spirit on my hands and with bare fingers I took the shrapnel out. As you can imagine, poking into the raw wounds with wide fingers inflicts lot more pain than sleek well-designed surgical instruments; that's why they are designed and manufactured!

Confession of a Terrorist!
Chapter 2   Jungle Camp

What is this 'pain' that we all experience? How does one describe 'pain' and how does one feel it? For thousands of years, across various cultures people accused of wrongdoing were made to walk on hot charcoals or plunge a hand in boiling water to prove that they are guiltless as God would protect the innocent! The township of Kataragama in the dense jungles of southeastern Sri Lanka (about 200 km from the capital city of Colombo) is a popular place of pilgrimage for the local Buddhist, Hindus and Moslems. The Tamil Hindus of Sri Lanka and south India refer to it as Katirkamam; the presiding deity is Lord Murugan or Skanda. Out of love for Lord Murugan and to assuage bad karma the faithful pierce their cheeks and tongues, and pull large chariots carrying the idol, with large hooks that have been pierced through the skin of their backs apparently not feeling any pain. During Thaipusam, a Festival of Thanks, Hindu pilgrims pierce their cheeks and tongues with metal skewers in sacred ritual evidently without feeling pain, in Singapore. Some Moslems of the Shi'a sect beat themselves on their back with metal chains, spikes and blades to mourn the brutal killing of Imam Hussain during the Islamic month of Muharram. And some devoted Christians practice self-flagellation and crucifixion during each Easter in the Philippines and

Confession of a Terrorist!
Chapter 2   Jungle Camp

Latin America. Don't they feel pain; and if not, why not?

All of the three young ladies were in attendance to provide nursing care to this boy Freedom Fighter who should be in agony. One had her hands on his forehead and caressing, another was stroking his face and cheek, and the third holding his hands trying to calm him down as there was no anesthesia. It worked better than anesthesia. Not only could I see no evidence of him feeling pain, but he was in seventh heaven; there were three beautiful 'city-girls' for one country-boy from a village in Noakhali; he was in heaven on earth! He did not have to die and go to heaven for his beautiful women; he was getting them all here on earth! And that speaks volumes for the non-traditional approaches to pain management such as acupressure, acupuncture, healing touch, hypnotism, reflexology etc.

After removing the shell fragments, I sutured his wounds. There was only one "ouch" and that too was muffled. He was faking a smile all the while through the procedure – another lesson in medicine that I did not learn in the medical college as to how subjective the sensation of pain can be!

Confession of a Terrorist!
Chapter 2 Jungle Camp

Based on the number of casualties we received at Sonamura, it seemed that the intensity of combat operations was not high; or perhaps it was and our Freedom Fighters were smart and/or fortunate enough not to take too much enemy fire. We used to get 2-3 patients a day, most of them from shrapnel (commonly from anti-personal mines) and bullet wounds. Fortunately, none were in life-threatening locations such as the chest or belly, mostly in the limbs. Then there were some medical cases with malaria, diarrhea and dysentery. Though malaria had been eradicated from East Pakistan by then - courtesy of the World Health Organization, it remained endemic here in Tripura; the dense jungles in Tripura were a favorite breeding place for the mosquitoes making it hard to stamp out. Patients with these latter (medical) conditions would come at the last moment; they wanted to be macho and "ride it out" as if through their disregard, it would make them go away. They did not want to waste time coming to the hospital for 'minor' ailments such as diarrhea or fever lest they miss any military or guerrilla action. All in all, the wounded and the sick Freedom Fighters who came to Sonamura enjoyed a very high patient to nursing care ratio.

This relative lull in combat injuries allowed us plenty of spare time which we made good use of,

Confession of a Terrorist!
Chapter 2   Jungle Camp

most often reading books, receiving and seeing-off Freedom Fighters transiting on their way, attending to various guests of whom there was no shortage, and visiting one or two Sub-Sector. Though my college-buddy Capt. Kabir had invited me to go visit his Sub-Sector Dhonpur a few times it never materialized for some reason or other. Capt. Mahboob's Nirvoypur Sub-Sector was one of the most active and a disproportionately large number our patients with combat injury were coming from there. One day Capt. Akhtar was going to visit Nirvoypur and tagged me along.

The jungle was dense and impenetrable here; the camp was on a hill and appeared like a giant complex of tree-houses! Again, something out of the movies or pictures that I have seen of the guerilla fighters in Vietnam, Laos and Kampuchea; it was as impressive as fascinating. Capt. Mahboob looked young for his age which could not have been much anyway. He had a boyish face with height and weight of an average Bengali. He had gentle manners, was very pleasant, but he was not vociferous, rather reserved perhaps he has some pent-up anger in him and that's understandable. Underneath all that docile appearance was a fierce tiger – an angry Royal Bengal; as intrepid as he is, under his command, his daring boys had harassed the

Confession of a Terrorist!
Chapter 2   Jungle Camp

Pakistan military the most, thereby taking the most hits from them in return, as one would expect. Capt. Mahboob was not a frequent traveler to our Rest-House. As I had just noted before, he was somewhat of a recluse; I don't recall seeing much of him afterwards.

Another day I took advantage of the relative quietness of patient-care activity and asked Gafoor to teach me how to drive the pickup van, of course with the permission of Capt. Akhtar. We felt that the road to Melaghor and on to Agartala would be a safe one to practice as there was very little traffic. Though I had been a motorcycle rider for 8 years by then, I did not know how to drive a car, save my first lesson back when I was 9 or 10. The road was narrow, barely allowing two cars to cross each other; when there was a bus or a truck one of the vehicles had to leave the pavement and be on the soft shoulder. The road was also elevated from the land about 2 m higher as that section of it was part of the embankment of the River Gomoti. Being part of the British Commonwealth (a euphemism for previous colony) in India the traffic pattern is similar to that in Pakistan, drive on the left side of the road. So, that was not difficult; but during my first run, I veered too much off to the right and ended up in the riverbank! It was a steep slope and the pickup van could have been overturned; Gafoor was scared, but I managed to bring the van back to the highway and after that, I got the hang of steering it and drove safely back to the hospital.

The Missionaries from Agartala

As in all warfare, spy business is an important part of military operations. The town of Sonamura being so close to the border and the Pakistan army bunkers within a km or so of the Rest-House Hospital, the Freedom Fighters were ever vigilant for anyone who might be Pakistani infiltrators, spies, saboteurs or other undesirable elements; there were no shortage of *Razakar* traitors either. Taher, Capt. Akhtar's Batman spotted a jeep with two nuns from a catholic mission in Agartala at the ferry *ghat*. It seemed that the missionaries were looking for a hospital here that they have heard of. It turns out that they had gone to the refugee camp on the south bank of the River Gomoti, not too far from the BSF (Border Security Force) position commanded by Maj. Chouhan. The refugee camp had several thousand people and the missionaries went there to deliver humanitarian aids including powdered milk, first-aids, vitamins, antibiotics and other medical supplies. The physician in charge of the medical

Confession of a Terrorist!
Chapter 2 Jungle Camp

care there was not available at the time [The *Mukti Bahini* and thus Capt. Akhtar was not responsible for the medical care of the refugee camps as that was undertaken by the government of India and the various relief organizations]. The missionaries did not want to take their gifts back to Agartala and so they thought that they might give it to us.

Taher met them at the ferry *ghat* and brought them to the Rest-House. I greeted them and instantly sent Taher to get some samosa, sweets etc.[4] It did not take these nuns long to figure out that we were Freedom Fighters. Their policy was only to give the aids to refugees and they were barred from giving it to political organizations. I exposed them to the meager facility we had (or did not have) with

---

[4] During the time prior to my joining the *Mukti Bahini*, I had tried to save as much money as I could so that I could support myself. My dad had left quite a large sum of money in the iron-safe to which I had a key. But I neither touched that, nor did I exchange them with new currency the Pakistan government had issued and declared the old to be useless within a specified time; it was a judgment-call; and retrospectively I was wrong; to great exasperation of my father and a deep sense of guilt in me, the money lost all of its value. Of my personal belongings was a Phillips electric shaver and a British-made Triumph Tiger Cub motorcycle which I sold off, took part of the proceeds in cash and converted the rest in 2 gold guineas. So when I arrived in Sonamura, I had some money I could use for good causes.

Confession of a Terrorist!
Chapter 2   Jungle Camp

very little medical supplies. I recounted the incidence that just a few days prior to their arrival I had taken the shrapnel out of the limb and abdominal wall of a Freedom Fighter with bare hands as there were no gloves and instruments. By the time we came back from the short tour of our medical "facility" tea was served and so was the delicious *rosh molai, sondesh, samsoa* (snacks) etc. I sensed that they liked the sweets [they had to, Sonamura was famous for its *rosh molai* just as those from Comilla], were touched by the lack of medical supplies and perhaps were softening their posture. After all, they are missionaries, they have hearts! I pleaded that neither were we a political organization, nor were we affiliated with any. I also argued that we too were refugees and therefore deserved their compassion. Without wishing to belittle the struggle and suffering of our fellow countrymen in the refugee camps, my final line of reasoning was that the only difference between we refugee and those in the camps is that we are doing something to end our disgraceful status and go back home as soon as possible. That did it! Hooray! Not only did they leave the whole jeep-load of supplies but invited me to visit them at their church in Agartala for future needs.

Confession of a Terrorist!
Chapter 2 **Jungle Camp**

Indian Military officers

The Indian Border Security Forces (BSF) outpost about 3-4 km south of Sonamura was commanded by Maj. Chouhan, a Rajput I believe. He too used to stop by our hospital, and pretty soon he did. That was the first time I met an Indian military officer. He was one of the nicest persons I had met. He was a perfect gentleman, polite, courteous and cultured. I subsequently had the privilege of meeting several other officers, up to the rank of Brigadier General and found each of them to be similar to Maj. Chouhan; what a contrast with the Pakistani military officers?! Forget the officers; in Pakistan, even the lowly sepoy (an ordinary soldier equivalent to a private in US military) had wielded so much power and arrogance that the civilians were made to feel like dirt no matter what their social status may have been.

As his routine, one day Maj. Chouhan came to the hospital and this time was specifically looking for Capt. Akhtar. There was an outbreak of diarrhea and dysentery in the refugee camp near his outpost, the doctor was not there and one or two of his troops had taken ill. He wanted us to help him, and specifically asked for me. He sugar-coated his request by telling that I could spend the night there and

Chapter 2   Jungle Camp

gain a firsthand experience in staying that close to the border and with an Indian paramilitary unit! That did not take long; we had no serious patients in the hospital and no casualties were expected from the area Sub-Sectors; Capt. Akhtar complied with his request to send me to his outpost. We left late afternoon.

We crossed the River Gomoti by ferry and drove south; the road from here on the south bank was unpaved but was surfaced with gravel. The terrain was similar to that on the north bank, small hills and valleys with little villages interspersed with dense jungles and rice paddy fields. To our right, on the west is the border, hardly a kilometer or less. Maj. Chouhan's BSF camp was at the western edge of the village Srimontopur; in other words, it was a buffer between the civilians in the village to the east and Pakistan Army position on the west. The BSF's equivalent of Pakistani Border defense (East Pakistan Rifles or EPR) had been dismantled; those who had revolted or escaped are now part of the *Mukti Bahini (Mukti Fouz)* along with those from the regular army unit. Hence these Pakistani border outposts, normally defended by EPR are now manned by the 'real men' of the regular Pakistan Army soldiers!

Confession of a Terrorist!
Chapter 2   Jungle Camp

The camp was sprawling with tents where the BSF soldiers lived, the front bunkers were further to the west; the Pakistan Army position in occupied Bangladesh is only a few hundred meters across the no-man's land from here. Because of the heightened tension and the risk of exchange of fire Maj. Chouhan did not want his guest on harm's way. I went to the refugee camp. It was a human tragedy of unbelievable proportion. There must have been at least 10,000 men, women and children huddled up in long rectangular bamboo houses. In this camp, the refuges were mostly if not exclusively were of Hindu faith and came from the villages in adjacent district of Comilla[5]. They lived in crammed quarters with extremely poor sanitary and hygienic conditions. Even though the Government of India and various aid agencies had been providing food and medicine, it was by no means adequate; I could clearly see signs of malnourishment in them.

---

[5] While working on this book I was doing some Internet research and to my utter disbelief and sorrow I came across postings which erroneously claim that the refugees were not from Bangladesh, rather they were plucked from the slums of Kolkata! The best I could tell, these refugees that I saw left their homes in Bangladesh, and not from India.

Confession of a Terrorist!
Chapter 2 Jungle Camp

The physician for the refugee camp was not there when I arrived; he was not posted there round-the-clock. After I had tended to some of the patients in the refugee camp and then seen Maj. Chouhan's boys, it was getting dark and the good Major insisted that I have supper with him. His offer was very sincere and genuine, and I could not decline his invitation. We had a nice meal; the Major was a vegetarian, but inquired whether I wanted a meat dish. I wanted to have a glimpse in the life of Maj. Chouhan, so a taste of his diet was perfect; I told him that I would eat whatever he will. It was a nice meal of *chapatti* (Indian flat bread) sautéed vegetable, *daal* (lentil) etc. A perfect gentleman and a great host, knowing that I am a Bengali, he asked me whether I wanted rice or not. Though I was sure the rice he was going to serve was of much better quality and especially without adulterated with gravel-chips, I politely declined; I did not want to remember the rice we eat in Sonamura that was a blend of 1-2% stone-chips, at least!

We had a nice long dinner; we chatted a lot, talked about ourselves, our family, the politics etc. He had an extra bed in his tent where I slept very comfortably as it was not the uneven wooden floor of the Rest-House; I did not have to use my boots to rest

Confession of a Terrorist!
Chapter 2 Jungle Camp

my head, I even had an air-pillow! I was overwhelmed by his hospitality.

CHAPTER 3

HUNTING TRIP

The morale of the young men fighting for the independence of their homeland is one of the most striking things about the *Mukti Bahini*, only being a close second to their determination. There was this young man popularly known as Gopi Kashem. He thought he was a Cliff Richard or Tom Jones – the then popular British singers of the 1960's and 1970's; Kashem had managed to bring his guitar with him and would sing at every opportunity, his favorite "...my sweet Delilah..." Besides the Laurel & Hardy type duo Bahar and Jamal who would constantly make us laugh as long as they were there, Kashem also entertained us with his songs. But since he did not sing the Bengali songs, it was

Confession of a Terrorist!
Chapter 3 Hunting Trip

somewhat uninteresting for those who did not appreciate him. He was not a bad singer, but he would not stop on his own unless he was virtually strangled! My medical college education and training in psychiatry was minimal, but it was possible that perhaps he was coping with the situation by singing. On the subject of psychiatry, without wishing to belittle any of my professional colleagues, I think the readers may be amused by this common gag in the medical community: "an internist knows everything, but does nothing; a surgeon knows nothing but does everything; a psychiatrist knows nothing and does nothing; and a pathologist knows everything and does everything but it's a day later!" And I know nothing of the discipline that itself knows "nothing!"

Jokes aside, it is not easy for young men who leave their parents, siblings, friends and neighbors, and the comfort and security of their homes to come to the jungles of another country to be trained to kill and be prepared to be killed, or worse tortured and then killed. Most of these boys, I should say suppressed their fear, anxiety, insecurity etc. or, pretended to suppress. Kashem was not pretending, perhaps he was letting it out through his voice till threatened with strangulation. Kashem had a tender heart and was in need of love and affection which he got a lot here at the hospital from his brotherly and sisterly elders. As astute and sensitive as Capt. Akhtar is, he made Kashem feel it at home here at the Rest-House; so he came here at every available opportunity; one almost felt that he was a permanent member of our hospital.

Paki (not pakhi[1]) Hunting

Though I am here to treat the sick and wounded and help save lives [in reality a life is never saved, we can merely prolong it, with relative comfort, more or less] being in the war-front it was imperative that I also have some training in using fire-arms in the event of a need. After all, we are dealing with Pakistani military, a fighting machine that uses religion to keep the country united only on that basis, a distance of 1600 km between the two parts notwithstanding. What happened to the rhetoric of *"toom vee mosalman, haam vee mosalman?"* Why are the supposed fellow innocent Muslim brothers being killed, sisters/mothers

---

[1] While Paki is short for Pakistani soldiers, a phonetically close word "pakhi" in Bānglā means bird.

Confession of a Terrorist!
Chapter 3　　　　　　Hunting Trip

being raped[2]? This is an enemy that has no morals, no scruples; they can never be trusted. Besides, the animal [or human - animals do not take revenge!] in me was looking for vengeance; several of my buddies were slaughtered whose parents and siblings were ordered to watch the execution, my middle-aged uncle - a totally innocent man was badly beaten, not to mention of an estimated 3 million other Bengalis who perished and 400,000 women raped that I do not know personally. I do not recall exactly who initiated; either I asked Capt. Akhtar or, he made the suggestion that I get some training in using light firearms. Almost immediately I was taken to the firing range where I target practiced with a Chinese submachine gun (SMG) modeled after the famous Russian AK-47[3]. By this time, thanks to the Freedom Fighters transiting through, I had already seen several different types of light firearms: the Indian self-loading

---

[2] An estimated 200,000-400,000 Bengali women were raped in Bangladesh by the Pakistanis in just 9 months. By comparison, 20 years later during 1992-1995, the rapes of about 20,000 Bosnian women forced the world to recognize **rape as "an instrument of terror," as a crime against humanity**. Where were the Western 'civilized democracies' in 1971? Do women have to be Western to be recognized as rape victims?
http://www.nytimes.com/2010/08/25/world/asia/25iht-letter.html.

[3] AK-47 was developed by Mikhail Kalashnikov, AK-47 stands for Kalashnikov Automatic rifle, model of 1947.

Confession of a Terrorist!
Chapter 3   Hunting Trip

rifle (SLR), the Indian submachine gun with short barrel that has cooling vents (for close combat), the Tommy gun, the 0.303 rifles etc.

A few days later in mid-July, one evening Capt. Akhtar was in a mood to do something naughty! His wife Khuku *vabi* had been sent to West Bengal to Capt. Akhtar's grandparents' house for safety a few days earlier (before my arrival); so he could afford to be mischievous and not be held back. He wanted to go hunting. His acquaintance Rumi – a young Freedom Fighter from Dhaka had jumped at the idea. Bahar and Jamal were even more enthused and so was Capt. Akhtar's Batman Taher. I had never gone hunting; as a matter of fact the only time I did something like that was when my youngest aunt (my dad's youngest sister) took me out to teach me fishing when I was about 4. I was so saddened to see those fishes jumping in agony and struggling for life, that I never ever went fishing again; it is bad enough I eat them, but I cannot stand the sight of them suffering. But inasmuch as I abhor killing or even hurting life, this evening I too wanted to go hunting! 'Cause we were going to hunt the Pakis! I wanted vengeance.

Confession of a Terrorist!
Chapter 3   Hunting Trip

Admittedly, I had no experience in combat; I only had learnt just a few days ago how to fire a submachine gun. Owing to my lack of combat experience, and being concerned about my safety and the safety of the rest of the hunting party Capt. Akhtar refused to include me; others too were discouraging me; that made me very sad. But how do you gain experience without doing it? I hear it time and time again "you are not qualified as you have no experience" and my answer to that has always been the same "I want to start gaining that experience from here, now" anytime I was given that excuse in various situations including my first interview at the University of Maryland in 1975 for entering into a career of doing biomedical research. But that was not the argument I dared use as the price of my gaining this experience right then and right there could cost one or more lives of my dear comrades. So, without a line of reasoning and therefore hope, I was very sad and made no attempt to hide it either. Capt. Akhtar was touched; reluctantly he assented with very strict condition that I obey every single order without question or hesitation, to which I readily agreed with enormous gratitude and ecstasy.

I was given a spare Indian submachine gun as they were in abundant supply from the Indian army; the more efficient and coveted Chinese submachine guns were limited as they were brought in by the revolting Bengali members of Pakistani armed forces. The Indian submachine guns had a shorter range and were more suitable for close combat than the Chinese ones of slightly longer range. Putting its strap on my shoulder and holding the handle with my right hand and the cold barrel with the left in position for action gave me a strong sense of power instantly. Realizing what was going on through my mind and body Capt. Akhtar however told me to cool off; for safety reason, he told me that I could cock the gun to fire only after he told me to do so.

Around 23:00 Hrs we started walking west along the embankment towards the border. Close to the border we got off the embankment, turned north and then due west, back again into the flat no-man's land. We walked for several kilometers deep inside Bangladesh in total darkness. Having left Bangladesh only a few days ago and going back inside in the darkness of night gave me an eerie feeling. It must have been between 01:00 and 02:00 Hrs. when we spotted a hut in the middle of nowhere with lights in it. With guns cocked, we raided the place; hilariously, it turned out to be a smugglers' den; several of them were

Confession of a Terrorist!
Chapter 3   **Hunting Trip**

playing cards and they, true to their profession vanished 'in thin air,' or shall we say in the darkness of the night!

Laughingly we walked back towards Sonamura again. This time first due south towards the embankment and back to the Rest-House. A few hours later the hunting party was ready again, this time along the embankment all the way to the Pakistan Army bunker position across the River Gomoti. The hunters were deployed on the north side of the embankment so that the embankment worked as a defensive shield from retaliatory enemy fire – the enemy was across the river on the south bank, in their bunkers hardly 200 m away. Then started the waiting game; it waited, and waited and waited till it was daybreak when two Bengali women were spotted coming out of the bunkers and walking along the river towards Bibir Bazaar. Soon after came out two *Pakis* (Pakistani military); our ambush party opened fire and immediately gunned them down. Thankfully, it was not I whose bullet did it though. The burst of automatic light-weapon fire continued at their position for a few more minutes. Expecting retaliation from the enemy with heavier firepower, especially since two of their comrades had been killed, the hunters retreated.

Confession of a Terrorist!
Chapter 3   Hunting Trip

It did not take long for the news to reach the Sector Head-Quarter in Melaghor. The next day Maj. Khaled Mosharraf and Maj. Nurul Islam (aka Shishu *vai* – later became Maj. General and a member of the Cabinet in independent Bangladesh) came over to the hospital. I was pleasantly surprised when Maj. Khaled Mosharraf showed concern about my safety and expressed his unhappiness at my participation by telling me "Doc, I have enough people to do the killing, but not enough to save them; I need you more here in the hospital than in the battle field." Maj. Nurul Islam's reaction was more of amuse; he seemed to have liked the idea that in our spare time we were inflicting some damage to the enemy.

The Air Force

One day around midmorning we had another visitor – a very handsome young man – smart and debonair. He was out of the ordinary. Almost everyone if not all of them from Bangladesh whom I had met before whether they were part of *Mukti Bahini* or not had this unshaven, disheveled, rugged appearance; even Maj. Khaled Mosharraf, his Hollywood/Bollywood looks and panache notwi-

Confession of a Terrorist!
Chapter 3   Hunting Trip

thstanding. This young man was clean-shaven, sophisticated and charming, as if he was walking into a Saturday night disco party. He was sporting a bright colorful (orange checkered with contrasting thin black or blue stripes) short-sleeve shirt that perfectly complimented his complexion, and with matching jeans that fit him well like a model walking out of the cover-page of a Men's style magazine. I have vivid recollection of his shirt as not only it was so striking but also very beautiful; a year or so later when in the United States I finally saw a similar one that I bought for myself which did not look half as good on me as it did on him. He introduced himself as Flight Lieutenant (Flt Lt) Nurul Kader, Commanding Officer of a Sub-Sector in Sector 4 (Sylhet area, Maj. Chitta Ranjan Datta Commanding Officer). The moment we saw each other, we recognized that we were classmates in high school (Technical High School, now Government Science College & School in Tezgaon, Dhaka). Flt Lt Nurul Kader (nicknamed Deedar) and I were buddies while we both attended Classes VI and VII 1958-1959. He liked singing, not as unrelenting as Kashem and his English songs, but popular Bengali and Hindi songs of those days; I was a good listener. While we were in Class VII he went to Pakistan Air Force Cadet School in Lower Topa and on to the Pakistan Air

Confession of a Terrorist!
Chapter 3   **Hunting Trip**

Force Academy in Risalpur, West Pakistan, became an air force pilot and now a member of the *Mukti Bahini*. We had not seen each other since then. Pakistani military was arresting the family members of any *Mukti Bahini* they could identify and track, subjected them to torture and eventually death. Everyone especially those who defected like Flt Lt Nurul Kader were gravely concerned about their family. His mother, a brother and sister lived in Comilla-Noakhali area; he came to meet them after they had safely crossed the border and arrived in Sonamura a few days prior.

I had fond memories of Nurul Kader; his mother liked me very much and would treat me to snacks every time I visited him. *Khalamma*[4] seemed to have remembered me after all these years and showed her love and affection as if not a day had passed. Reminiscing our old friendship Flt Lt Nurul Kader invited me to serve in his Sub-Sector which I believe was in Kukital, Karimgonj area, about 50-60 km from Shilchar in the Indian state of Assam. That was a very attractive proposition. Him being my first close childhood friend that I

---

[4] *Khalamma* refers to an elder Moslem woman, sister or friend of one's mother; also used commonly to refer to friend's mothers. The equivalent salutation for Hindu women logically is *Mashi* from *Ma* (mother).

Confession of a Terrorist!
Chapter 3   Hunting Trip

encountered here, I told him that he will not have to 'twist my arm' for me to move there. Soon after he had a very emotional reunion with his family he left for his Sub-Sector; he did not want to waste a minute in his effort to fight the enemy.

A few days later came another ex-Pakistan Air Force Officer; this time it was a Squadron Leader (Sq. Ldr. equivalent to a Major in the Army). He too was a Sub-Sector commander, but in Sector 6 (Rongpur-Dinajpur area, Wing Commander Khademul Bashar Sector Commander), and came to find out about his family stranded inside the Pakistan-occupied territory; he too was gravely concerned about his family back home and was apprehensively waiting for them to be smuggled across the border in this area. He had two sons, one 2 years of age and the other barely 3 months old. By now the Pakistan military knows that he is a Sub-Sector commander of the resistance; torturing his beloved wife and children is virtually guaranteed. At around 170 cm or less, with French-cut beard and sporting a sweet smile he was a typical Bengali. The mild manners of Sq. Ldr. Sadruddin Hossain clearly belie the fierce fighting spirit in this man. He would not talk much about his family; he was quite good in suppressing his feelings and never showed his fearfulness; instead he was trying to be upbeat, but knowing what he must have been going through was just as painful to us; we felt his pain.

Graduating the Terrorists!

Sq. Ldr. Sadruddin Hossain, by now has become our Sadru *vai*. As a distraction from his anxiety and worries about his beloved family, he kept himself busy by observing us, telling jokes or making some up and like. He was a keen observer; it appeared that he liked me and admired my work. He told me that his Sub-Sector was Dinajpur and that it was in the liberated parts of Bangladesh. When he saw expression of disbelief in my face that he was operating inside free Bangladesh, he asked me whether I knew of Tetulia. Tetulia is the northernmost town that appears in the common maps of East Pakistan or Bangladesh and of course I knew it. The southernmost point is Teknaf; these are often commonly used reference points to describe our land: "Teknaf to Tetulia." He told me that not only Tetulia is free of enemy but also the Sector Commander's family lives there. In order to entice me he also told me that being in liberated parts of our motherland, it feels different, the air smells fresh, the fish and vegeta-

Confession of a Terrorist!
Chapter 3   Hunting Trip

bles are tastier etc., etc. The bottom line, would you come to Sector 6? Apparently there was a civilian physician in private practice, a middle aged gentleman who was taking care of the Freedom Fighters there; but Sq. Ldr. Sadruddin wants more.

It was time that a large group of Freedom Fighters had finished their training and is ready to go inside East Pakistan to carry out their operations: blow bridges, cut off the train tracks, ambush Pakistani soldiers, grenade attacks etc. – terrorist activities on the vastly superior mighty Pakistani military. Following completion of their training there is a graduation ceremony in Melaghor.

The ceremony started at night fall in the jungles. There was the usual sentry post, but the atmosphere inside was different this evening as opposed to the first time I came when it was very serious; this evening it was a strange combination of being both solemn and festive! The tall trees were majestically reaching the sky making it look almost a small hole like we were in the bottom of a deep well. There were torches (*moshal*), hajack lamps,

Confession of a Terrorist!
Chapter 3   Hunting Trip

The Various Sectors of Liberation War

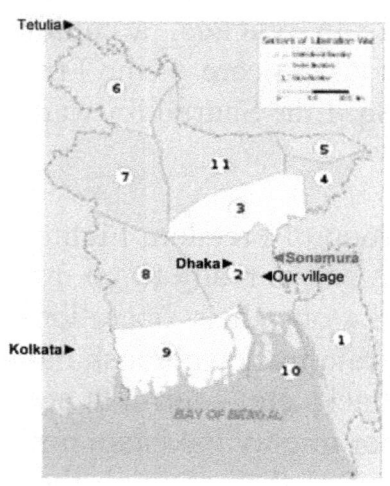

- My first trip was from Dhaka to Sonamura in Sector 2. Flt Lt Nurul Kader was from Sector 4 (Major Datta Commanding) and Sqdrn Ldr Sadruddin was from Sector 6 under Wing Com Bashar; in Tetulia resided Commander Bashar's wife and two daughters.

The strategic and tactical division of Bangladesh into 11 sectors of war-front[5]

kerosene lamps etc. The Freedom Fighters were walking in this semi-dark environment which was somber; it all appeared surreal. A stage was erected for the formal speeches, recitations etc. There were a couple of rows of folding chairs for both Bangladeshi and Indian military officers; I was privileged to be included amongst them and had a seat in the front row. It seemed like out of the movies.

---

[5] http://en.wikipedia.org/wiki/Bangladesh_Liberation_War d

Confession of a Terrorist!
Chapter 3   Hunting Trip

There were brief speeches, recitation of our National Anthem *"Amaar Shonar Bangla..."* (Oh My Golden Bengal How I love Thee...) and other patriotic songs and revolutionary poems from rebel-poet Kazi Nazrul Islam and others. It was very touching. No sooner the National Anthem ended, girls (Lulu, Tulu and Daliah) sitting nearby were sobbing in emotion. Sitting next to the girls was Sq. Ldr. Sadruddin. He had been making small talks and joking with the girls; I was sitting next to him on the other side. He told us that he had not only showered but had shampooed his hair for this special occasion, etc.

During the 1965 Pakistan-India war, Sq. Ldr. Sadruddin's fighter jet and other Pakistan Air Force Fighters were engaged in a dogfight with Indian Air Force planes. His aircraft was shot down by 'friendly-fire'; he had safely ejected off the cockpit and landed what he knew was inside Pakistan. As safe as his landing may have been, he was far from harm's way when the villagers found him. Not being fluent in Urdu or Panjabi the villagers took him for the Indian enemy pilot and mercilessly beat him up. Only after he was taken to the nearest police station following repeated pleas did the beating stop.

Confession of a Terrorist!
Chapter 3 Hunting Trip

Soon at the corner of my eyes I see this cheerful but otherwise tough and fearless Air Force fighter pilot who had survived being shot down from his fighter plane and then ruthless beating by the mob, wiping his eyes. This is the same man who just a few minutes beforehand were jovial, telling jokes. Was he trying to hide his emotion? I too tried to play cool, but to no avail; I could not hold back my tears either. When it was over, there was hardly anyone who did not have tears in their eyes. The national anthem, the patriotic songs, the induction of these tender-age volunteers who will be going on very dangerous missions tomorrow from where they may not come back alive, the dream that through these efforts we will become free again, all of these were powerful reasons not to be unemotional.

The next day some of our friends and acquaintances from Dhaka were going back there for commando operations. They graciously asked us what we needed from back home. We all could have our requests. I had come with some cash money, a couple of gold guineas each worth about 130 Indian Rupees then, a couple of pairs of jeans, a few shirts including one that Daliah had brought from Jakarta Indonesia during her trip as a part of cultural delegation a few months prior, and other

Confession of a Terrorist!
Chapter 3   Hunting Trip

bare necessities to survive in the jungle. I told them that I did not need anything from Dhaka. First, I really did not need anything; I wasn't here on holidays or pleasure; I could live by what bare essentials I brought with me. Secondly, I did not want anyone from the *Mukti Bahini* show up at my parents doors lest they are followed by the *Razakar* spies. That would mean definite torture and/or execution of my parents. One of the Freedom Fighters – Habibul Alam, insisted. I yielded reluctantly though and requested that they bring me my Cecil & Loeb's Text book of Medicine. They looked at me as if I was from a different planet, a text book of Medicine and nothing else?! Capt. Akhtar looked with disbelief as Cecil & Loeb during those days was a single volume very large and heavy book (2,000+ pages); about double if not triple the volume of the standard UK medicine text books for us in Dhaka Medical College. Cecil & Loeb was an American Text Book and I was very fond of it; that was the one I had been studying more in preparation of my ECFMG - the qualifying examination given to physicians worldwide for equivalency in USA. I had also been somewhat curious and aside from prescribed Text Books from UK, studied text books from Russia as well; it was quite educational. I however found the US text books quite informative and easy to read and comprehend. So I was naturally gravitated to them. Furthermore, since it was my childhood dream to be a scientist and USA was the leading country for scientific learning and research, I was preparing myself to go to USA for higher education; a natural first step was to be attuned to their line of thinking and education.

Half-jokingly Capt. Akhtar told them that my request would cost them enormous hardship. To that they simply responded "not a problem at all!" I was amazed; here we are worrying about the safety and life of these friends not knowing whether they will be able to come back alive or not, yet they are unfazed. Not only they did not seem to care about that, but they were also so very confident that they will be back and with all our requests fulfilled no matter how small or bulky they may be! It was like sitting in a restaurant, placing your dinner order and the well-experienced senior wait staff smilingly obliges; what self-confidence and bold determination!

Rain of Cluster Bombs

That Sonamura became a Freedom Fighters' safe-haven was no secret; the Pakistani military was

Confession of a Terrorist!
Chapter 3   Hunting Trip

well aware of it. Besides, we were becoming a nuisance to them, raiding their positions, killing them especially after they had finished raping Bengali women etc. It was also no secret that we had the full support and blessings of the people of Sonamura. They figured out that if they would terrorize the population, then the people of Sonamura would not be in support of us anymore and we would be forced out. Thus, courtesy of the Pakistan Army, mid-day on the 26th of July, it started to rain of Cluster Bombs[6] throughout the town of Sonamura. We heard this whooshing sounds that would be coming from the west, as it came overhead it stopped for a moment with eerie silence followed by explosion of the bomb canis-

---

[6] Cluster Bombs are literally hell from above. They are either air-dropped or ground-launched bombs that eject smaller sub-munitions i.e. cluster of bomblets (about the size of hand grenades) designed to kill enemy personnel and destroy vehicles. Cluster bombs release many small bomblets over a wide area. Therefore they pose risks to civilians both during and after the attacks. During attacks the weapons cause indiscriminate and wanton destruction, especially in populated areas. One in four secondary bomblets does not explode and if stays on the ground can explode on contact, usually with curious children. Unexploded bomblets can kill or maim civilians long after a shelling and the conflict has ended; the unexploded sub-munitions are expensive to locate and remove. There has been an international outcry for a long time to ban the use of Cluster Bombs. Pakistan happened to be one of the top 5 countries that use Cluster Bombs.

Confession of a Terrorist!
Chapter 3   Hunting Trip

ters low in the sky releasing the hundreds of secondary bomblets that would in turn explode sounding like popcorns popping to showers of hundreds if not thousands of shrapnel. These are reminiscent of the Chinese firecrackers except being menacing and deadly. The boom-boom sound of regular artillery fire seemed muffled and farther away than they really were. Instead, after a moment of spine-chilling silence, as the primary bombs explode overhead low in the sky; there was this scary screeching sound of the secondary bomblets now exploding that stabs through your heart to evoke absolute horror. What an effective terror machine! Realizing that the Pakistani military definitely know about our Rest-House being the hangout place and fearing that they might target it with conventional artillery shells, we instantly left the Rest-House and moved towards the pond in the back. Since the Rest-House was the westernmost building at the edge of Sonamura there was nothing but open space west of it towards the border; so it could take a direct hit from the Pakistani artillery.

There were a couple of patients who were not in too serious a condition; they too came out towards the pond. The rest of the inhabitants of Sonamura were in total panic; they were fleeing in any direc-

Confession of a Terrorist!
Chapter 3   Hunting Trip

tion they could, and in the process their good-feelings towards us evaporating instantaneously. Pretty soon the whole town was deserted, it looked like a ghost town; I have seen those only in the Hollywood Western movies, the "Spaghetti Westerns" just before the bandits were coming to town to kill, rape and loot. The only difference was that in those Hollywood Westerns the townspeople were hiding in their homes or shops; in Sonamura they left their homes, their shops, the bazaar, just as our refugees have been doing for the past 3+ months. Sadly but effectively, perhaps now they will be able to have an appreciation of how it feels to flee ones' home in terror.

We certainly felt very guilty that the people of Sonamura were at risk only because of our presence there. It is bad enough that India was hosting by then close to 10 million refugees from Bangladesh and the Indian citizens were paying a special Refugee Tax to support them; but to put their life at risk? That was not acceptable, neither was it okay to put our own lives at risk. Here is an example of the farsightedness of a brilliant military leader; apparently Major Khaled Mosharraf and others at the Head-Quarter were anticipating this and they already had a spot about 8 km in the interior, in the middle of a jungle as an alternate spot

Confession of a Terrorist!
Chapter 3 Hunting Trip

for the hospital. The shelling of Cluster Bombs went on for quite some time; I had lost track of time; it must have gone on for about an hour if not more. Or, perhaps not, it may have seemed that long as we just could not wait for it to stop. Then suddenly we started to hear some thunderous sounds of artillery fire nearby to the north, it was the Indian Army's answer. The Cluster Bombs stopped raining over us, not in a diminuendo fashion but abruptly, just the way it started, and only after the Indian Artillery retaliated with some heavy bombardment of their own on the Pakistani Army positions.

One has to give credit to the Pakistani Military; their strategy worked: Terrorize the innocent population of an entire town with Cluster Bombs and they will turn against the enemy they have been sheltering – collective punishment. Pakistani military government under Lt General Tikka Khan had been practicing this collective punishment on the Bengalis for some time, destroying the houses of minorities especially Hindus, suspected Freedom Fighters, politicians of any level and stature, local community leaders, students and student leaders, intellectuals etc.; but collective punishment of civilians in another country? How blatant an aggression can be aside from being cowardice!

Confession of a Terrorist!
Chapter 3   Hunting Trip

Capt. Akhtar happened to be at the HQ in Melaghor during this time; he soon appeared with an order for us to move out! We would be outside the range of Pakistani artillery, at least for the time being; destination: *Darogar Tilla*. This is exactly a month from my first arrival to Sonamura on the 27th of June.

CHAPTER 4

TENT HOSPITAL

I have no idea how the name *Darogar Tilla* came from, but this became our home for exactly a month, 27 July to 26 August! The Bengali word *Darogar* means "of a *Daroga* (an Officer-in-Charge of a police station, or the local Chief of Police)". This is a hillock (*Tilla*) about 2-3 km from the Sector 2 Head-Quarter in Melaghor along the Agartala road; the crow-flight distance could be shorter. The hillock may have belonged to the local Chief of Police, but I never found out. One had to travel a hundred meters or so from the road to reach the foot of the hillock. It seemed that it was larger than a *tilla* but smaller than a hill. Be that as it may, it was high and pretty steep. It was also the monsoon

Confession of a Terrorist!
Chapter 4   Tent Hospital

season and rain was heavy with the only access road to the top being deeply muddy. Only 4-wheel drive jeeps could make it to the top; sometimes it was so bad that even they would not be able to come up to the top! I recall seeing Maj. Khaled Mosharraf leaving his Toyota 4-wheel drive jeep at the bottom of the hill and walking up, with style of course! Unlike everyone else, he would lock his knees in full extension, bend his ankle about 30º and with straight back he would be coming up; he looked pretty cool. I tried his method; flexing the ankle allowed me to dig the heel of my boots in the mud giving me better traction as I was climbing uphill. I'm not sure if I looked quite as chic but I could feel an advantage.

The top of the hill was relatively flat like a plateau and not conical as one would have expected; it was also free of large trees, more or less. This meant that a) the leadership i.e. Maj. Mosharraf and Capt. Akhtar had chosen the site carefully and b) we did not have to go through a lot to setup our tents; simply the shrubs had to be removed. By the time we arrived at the top, all of that was done and more. Seven or eight large tents were already erected and a few smaller ones. Two of the large tents were for patients, one for male physicians and officers except Capt. Akhtar who as commander of the hospital and having his beloved wife Khuku with him [Khuku *vabi* returned from West Bengal the week before] had a small private tent. There was a large tent for the women who volunteered nursing services; the other large tents were for material storage, medical & surgical supplies, outpatient clinic etc. Cooking was done in the open air by digging a hole in the ground and using the firewood which was in abundant supply in the jungle around us.

The only source of water was a well in the bottom of the hill where we would also shower. Having taken the shower we would be walking uphill in that hot and muggy weather to the top; as you can imagine we were drenched in sweat by the time we came back to the tents. The cooks had to carry buckets of water all the way up the hill for cooking and drinking. It was quite arduous. Naturally, other activities that could be done at the foothill such as washing clothes were down below by the well. There was a separate shower area for the girls.

The young ladies did not restrict their activity solely in providing nursing care (or superfluous care as in Sonamura where there was a 3:1 nurse to patient ratio). They supervised the cooks to make sure that they did a good job, acted as Public Relations personnel when we had visiting dignitaries etc.

The Mosquito Militia

At nightfall we could hear the wild life - the foxes, the jackals, the owls etc. Because of the abundance of Royal Bengal tigers in the Sundarbon area [in the past], Bengali children grow up fearing of 'tigers in the jungle'. Thus, in the midst of this jungle, presumed threat of tigers was not an unreasonable concern even though there were none as far I could tell. But that had not stopped the girls from being scared since in the city they never heard these sounds. They were even more scared as their tents were to the northwestern edge of the campus, closer to the jungle where it seemed that the foxes and jackals were howling very near the tents. The cooking area was also at the western edge and near the girls' tent. Presumably the leftover food items that were trashed also served as a major attraction for these wild animals, though the girls dreaded it was them the jackals were after!

In the tent that was assigned for me to sleep, the floor was of course the leveled bare earth covered with *Hogla* mats (mats woven from the sturdy bark of tall slender shrubs) that served as our beds. At nightfall, the mosquitoes were everywhere, only second to the air we breathed; at the beginning their

Confession of a Terrorist!
Chapter 4   Tent Hospital

cacophony made it difficult to fall asleep. We had put the mosquito repellents at work. Along with the fact that I did not have enough sets of clothes, and the nights being hot and muggy I was sleeping with scanty clothes. The next morning I saw that the mat was polka dotted with red. It seemed that after the battalion of mosquitoes had feasted on my blood, they were too heavy to fly away and as I had tossed and turned they were crushed by my body. I looked at the mat where Sq. Ldr. Sadruddin was sleeping, it was the same. The mosquito repellents were not good enough to keep them at bay. So an urgent order of business was to protect ourselves with heavier clothing that would cover most of our body. That meant sleeping with thick jeans, full-sleeve shirts, socks and boots on; luckily, we received some air-pillows from the Head-Quarter Supplies, so we could sleep at night with our boots on. After using my boots as pillow for a whole month, that air-pillow was a luxury. I bought the appropriate clothes on my next trip to Agartala for medicine from the Missionaries. Thanks to Dr. Roy Choudhury and the Indian Red Cross who provided me with a monthly salary, I could buy the necessary clothing, rather camping gears! So, after my arrival in the USA when my friends and acquaintances invite me to go camping, I politely decline. When they insist, I tell them that I had enough camping experience of a lifetime; thank you! I prefer the comfort of my home.

While I was fortunate to get a stipend and buy my bare necessities, not everyone was as lucky. Evidently many Freedom Fighters did not receive any money although they were supposed to; some received a partial amount and irregularly. Most Freedom Fighters from Dhaka had brought in their own funds from home; whereas most of those from the rural areas did not. Not that they expected a salary when they voluntarily signed up to fight for their country, but knowing that they were entitled to it and not receiving it was demoralizing besides causing hardship. But that did not seem to deter their fighting spirit though.

The tents for patients could accommodate 6-8 each; that meant that we had increased our bed-capacity by 4 to 5-fold. By sheer coincidence or by design, the number of patients we were receiving started to climb as if they needed to fill the empty beds. It seemed that the combat operations in various sub-sectors had heated up dramatically; our Freedom Fighters and their commanders were getting impatient, and since we now have better capability to tend to their wounds, why not gear up the activity?!

Confession of a Terrorist!
Chapter 4　　　　　　Tent Hospital

Local Health Center

On a relatively quiet day I had the privilege of visiting the local Health Center in Melaghor which was equivalent to the Rural Health Clinics in erstwhile East Pakistan although the facility here is several times larger. I was impressed and amazed by not only the physical structure, but also the quality of medical service offered to the citizens. There were two MBBS physicians and a senior physician with postgraduate training in Kolkata; one junior physician was on-call around the clock. The Postgraduate Institutes in Dhaka in East Pakistan or Karachi in the West were in their infancy. The West Pakistani physicians and other professionals were at liberty to travel abroad; they could easily go to UK or USA for higher education and training; a fact I confirmed by the plethora of them in Baltimore. When I arrived in Massachusetts USA about 6 months following the Victory Day, I was the only one from the former East Pakistan amongst a group of 60 physicians from all over the world; in contrast, there were 6-7 from West Pakistan! A year later I arrived in Baltimore, Maryland and again, besides me, there were two other Bengali physicians as opposed to nearly 40 from West Pakistan all of whom have been in practice for at least 5 years following another 4-5 years of training, which

Confession of a Terrorist!
Chapter 4   Tent Hospital

points to the fact that they have been coming here since a long time. Now, consider the fact that the majority (56%) of the total Pakistani population was from the East; whereas the proportion of physicians training abroad was 1:6 to 1:12 for East *v* West Pakistan; these two samples show the glaring disparity.

We, in East Pakistan were simply not allowed to leave the country; we were required to stay in; for us to leave the country, we had to have a NOC (<u>N</u>o <u>O</u>bjection <u>C</u>ertificate) from the appropriate ministry. What step-motherly treatment, what discrimination?! Is this one country or is it a colony of West Pakistan?! We knew about the "Iron Curtain" in the Eastern European communist countries. But did the world know of the Iron Curtain surrounding East Pakistan? As if that was not bad enough, while travelling to West Pakistan in 1969 I had noted another disgusting behavior by the Pakistan Government. While I was flying from Dhaka Airport to Lahore in West Pakistan, I had to go through the Customs, but was not asked any question. However, on my return from West Pakistan, I and the rest of the members of my group were interrogated and our luggage searched by the Customs! Why do citizens of a country have to go through Customs Inspection when travelling *within* the same coun-

Confession of a Terrorist!
Chapter 4   Tent Hospital

try? And worse, why the Customs inspection is one way and not both ways? In other words, one could take anything and as much from East Pakistan to West, but you are restricted from bringing valuables from West Pakistan to East!

My most favorite uncle (my mother's brother) had lived in Karachi, West Pakistan for a long time and would come home once a year. When he used to tell us about the restrictions on goods coming from the West to East, we erroneously assumed that he was making it up so that he did not have to bring more gifts for us. Little did we know that to be the fact! Then there were news of people caught "smuggling" gold from West Pakistan to the East; smuggle within your own country?! Why would it be illegal to take perfectly legitimate goods from one part of the country to the other and only one-way?

I could not help but wonder: what was the purpose for this discrimination against us Bengalis when we were supposed to be 'one nation' through the fallacy of Islamic brotherhood? When combined with the 24 years of economic exploitation, the one way restriction of flow of goods and valuables, and restriction on higher education and training for us by not allowing us to go abroad point to a well-plan-

Chapter 4   Tent Hospital

ned and well-executed policy of keeping us inferior. The best way the Pakistan central government could dominate over us is to deny us the rights for better education, free travel etc.; its few Bengali abettors simply went along and served the new masters with enthusiasm. It must have been their grand scheme to make us inferior citizens. We may have been living in the fools' paradise of one country; to the Pakistan Government, we were simply their colony[1]. On 23 September 1932, the firebrand

---

[1] In August 1947 Pakistan was created by carving out the western and eastern parts of India 1,600 km apart as they had Moslem majority population. The former East Bengal became East Pakistan and the current day Pakistan as West Pakistan, the only factor connecting the two was the predominance of Islam as the religion; the language, culture and even the physical characteristics were completely different, as distant as the two parts. While the population in East Pakistan constituted 56% of the total, the West held the lion share of the economic, political and military power. In economic development alone, even though the East had the majority of population, only a fourth of the total national expenditure was in East Pakistan
(http://en.wikipedia.org/wiki/Six_point_movement). There was systematic discrimination against the Bengalis in every other front possible. While Bengali was the mother-tongue of the majority (56%), we were told that Urdu would be the national language, an extreme form of insult that was absolutely unacceptable. The Language Movement started in 1952 with the killing of unarmed student protestors on 21 February (proclaimed as the International Mother Language Day by UNESCO http://en.wikipedia.org/wiki/International_Mother_Language_Day). Subsequent uncorrected discrimination culminated in

Confession of a Terrorist!
Chapter 4   Tent Hospital

female Freedom Fighter Pritilata Waddedar had led the team of 10-12 men to attack the Pahartali Railway (European) club in Chittagong where there was a sign "Dogs and Indians not allowed" and not to fall behind, the Pakistanis too had their own sign later in the same club: "Dogs and Bengalis not allowed."

The trend in East Pakistan for those who wished higher medical education and training following MBBS was to aspire to go to UK for postgraduate education resulting in degrees such as FRCS, FRCOG and MRCP for surgery, gynecology and medicine respectively, of course after receiving the NOC. The American education and training was not looked upon favorably; I suppose as a bastion of capitalism, it was the common perception that people go to USA only to make money, implied is the statement that the training and education is not

---

political uprising in 1970; East Pakistanis (Bengalis) secured a majority of the seats in the national assembly. The military ruler General Yahya Khan postponed the opening of the national assembly in an attempt to circumvent East Pakistan's demand for greater autonomy. As a consequence, East Pakistan seceded and the independent state of Bangladesh, or Bengali nation, was proclaimed on 26 March 1971 the day after the beginning of the genocide.
(http://www.infoplease.com/ipa/A0107317.html?pageno=2, http://en.wikipedia.org/wiki/Bangladesh)

Confession of a Terrorist!
Chapter 4   Tent Hospital

worth going there. On the other hand, those four- or five-lettered degrees from our first colonial masters in UK were the tickets for higher positions, professorship in medical colleges and with that prestige, power and eventually wealth to the delight of your parents and relatives. If you knew someone at higher levels in the government that is, if you had an "uncle" then you are the most fortunate one to be eligible for a handful of government scholarships to go to UK or, to get the NOC relatively easily. On the other hand, for the vast majority it was a challenge, a lot of hard work, a lot of running around, plus bribery. Most who succeeded in making through our iron curtain stayed in UK, a fraction came back to become professors – usually those who were privileged to begin with, in getting the few scholarships available to Bengalis. But the number of professorial positions was extremely limited. So, there was little incentive for the UK-trained physicians to come back to East Pakistan.

The nascent Bangladesh Government had blindly adopted the same policy from East Pakistan unwittingly, not knowing or caring to know that the policy of NOC for Bengali professional was an instrument for systematic discrimination to keep us as second class citizens. Following the complete independence of the country when I was trying to

Confession of a Terrorist!
Chapter 4   Tent Hospital

go to USA to pursue my lifelong dream of becoming a scientist [I never wanted to be a physician, that was Dad's wishes and diktat], I had to go through the stumbling blocks of getting the NOC, for without that one could not even get a passport to leave the country. I cannot tell you how many people I had approached in vain; the worst were those whom I had mistaken as my benefactors and in position of power who could have helped but chose not to.

Dr. T. Hussain who became the Secretary of Health following the independence of Bangladesh had visited us here in our tent hospital at *Darogar Tilla*. During his inspection of our facility he had some very kind words for me as well as words of encouragement. He told me to see him after the independence for any help he could offer. He was gracious when I paid him a visit in his office at the Secretariat; but that was all; he would not give me a NOC which was within his power. And that was not all; some other presumed benefactors even threatened me that they will report me to the authorities for trying to leave the country! Ironically, the same characters several years later hypocritically and ashamedly were asking me for the favor of helping their children go to the USA! Paradoxically, help came from the corners least expected. An acquaint-

Confession of a Terrorist!
Chapter 4   Tent Hospital

tance of mine - Salahuddin Chowdhury, two years junior to me whom I do not recall even talking to him before he had approached me and offered to help get me a passport, totally unsolicited; it was a godsend. Though passport I got, NOC was not given to me; and that's another story. Fortunately, millions of thanks to Salahuddin and his brother Mr. Nazem Chowdhury – a high ranking government official, who had kindly instructed the then Director of Passport to issue me one "Travel Permit"[2]; I applied for it barely two or three days before I became a doctor, and hence technically I was still a student – meaning I did not need a NOC! Ironically Ehsanur Rahman, my classmate and friend who did not believe in this 'miracle' (Salahuddin was a bit different) tagged along. As Mr. Nazem Chowdhury was writing the instructions on a 5x7 cm notepad, Ehsanur implored him for one for himself; smilingly Mr. Nazem Chowdhury complied. Given the hardship that I and most others have endured, Ehsanur the lucky devil got it much too easily! The two of us then rushed to the Passport Office a few minutes before its closure for the day and the weekend. That 5x7 cm piece of paper was so powerful that the Director of Passport was pro-

---

[2] As a nascent country, The Peoples' Republic of Bangladesh did not have a passport during the early days. I was given a one-page legal-size paper "Travel Permit" which served as my passport.

fusely apologizing for his inability to issue us the passport that day owing to the lateness of the hour! Diffidently he asked "would it be okay if you receive them on Monday?" And then he asked me to my utter surprise "how is your father?" Little did I remember that Oh yes, Mr. Bahauddin, the Director was one of Dad's patients! After all, I probably could have received it only if I had asked my dad. Or, maybe not! I have heard and read of the trials and tribulations of the people from former communist countries trying to go abroad; the hurdles that I had to overcome were no less challenging.

In contrast in India, specifically in West Bengal and Tripura I was told that the excellent postgraduate education in Kolkata, Delhi, Bangalore and other major cities coupled with the benevolent system of public healthcare and other ancillary infrastructure, the higher trained physicians not only stay in the country, but the salary and other incentives make them go to remote places such as Melaghor. Of course, they are also free to go anywhere in the world for higher education; many of whom opt to stay abroad and many do return. One of the biggest incentives of all for a physician is however the opportunity and the facilities to provide the best care; as far I could see, the Government of India had provided that even in this remote place.

Confession of a Terrorist!
Chapter 4   Tent Hospital

During my short visit to West Punjab and the Northwest Frontier Province of West Pakistan, I had not had the opportunity to visit their rural health centers. So, I cannot make a fair and valid comparison with those in East Pakistan or India. But based on the progress I have seen in the faraway villages in Punjab such as electrification and paved roads and other telltale evidence of development, it would not be unreasonable to say that in East Pakistan we were getting a bad deal insofar as health care for the masses is concerned. Thus, while I was surprised to have seen a highly trained senior physician in the government health care facility in a remote place here in Melaghor, I could see the reason – the result of great healthcare planning by a munificent system of government that truly cares about its people.

Procuring Medicine and Other Medical Supplies

The increased patient traffic put a heavy demand on our medicines, surgical instruments, catheters and other supplies. Capt. Akhtar in the meantime had arranged for some to be bought through the regular *Mukti Bahini* Supplies. But that was barely sufficient. I took up the offer of the Missionaries in

Confession of a Terrorist!
Chapter 4   Tent Hospital

Agartala to get some more, and of course stealing from GB Hospital with Dr. Roy Choudhury as accomplice was always there. The supplies I managed from the Catholic Missionaries were mostly from Australia, some from UK; there were Johnson & Johnson Band-Aids, sterile gauzes, disposable syringes and needles, intravenous fluids and lines, almost everything a hospital in the developed country uses; oh yes, sterile disposable gloves; and a lot of them! These were distinctly different. Either the supplies themselves were colorful or the packages they were in were attractive, and state of the art in contrast to the reusable syringes and needles and other ancillary articles wrapped in drab paper. Interestingly, having wasted millions and millions of tons of these vital supplies, papers etc. and having destroyed our environment globally, 40 years later we are back to recycling to save the planet; hope it's not too late!

The Missionaries however had their routines and as expected were disciplined. They had followed quite rigid schedules and one simply could not walk up to them and get an audience as most businesses were [and still are] conducted in this part of the world. Most importantly the world could come to an end, but they could not be bothered while they are taking their siesta. We certainly did not have

Confession of a Terrorist!
Chapter 4 Tent Hospital

any telephone that we could communicate with and those were the days when there were no mobile phones that are omnipresent now-a-days. Travel to Agartala would be over an hour's trip. After taking care of the patients [I was the only physician taking care of them all as Capt. Akhtar had to be away most of the time coordinating the various activities; remember, he was in charge of medical care for the whole sector!] and handling all anticipated patient-complications for the rest of the day, it would be 10:00 or 11:00 Hr. by the time we would start for Agartala. We would be lucky if we could catch the Priest in the church before he went for lunch and siesta; if not, we would have to wait till 15:30 or 16:00 Hr. The church was outside the town of Agartala and way off our travel route. Thus often times, we had no choice but to wait patiently till the right time. We would most graciously accept their gifts and hurry back to the hospital.

Owing to the increase in patient-bed capacity, dramatic increase in the number of patients and increased and efficient procurement, we were well stocked in our Medical Supply tent, which was occasionally left unattended as a) there was not enough manpower and b) who would steal from us – the thieves who themselves have stolen or procured by begging these? But I started to suspect that some

Confession of a Terrorist!
Chapter 4   Tent Hospital

specific items were getting depleted faster than the rate of our use. What's going on? Whom to suspect?

The composition of visitors had changed since we moved to *Darogar Tilla*. Since it was not along the transit route of the Freedom Fighters and was on the opposite direction, they were not coming anymore. Word got around about the impressive nature of the Tent Hospital, so officials representing the Bangladesh government in exile were frequent visitors; it was a showcase of Sector 2. Various members of the Indian Military reconnaissance teams would be passing by. Officers ranking from Captain to Brigadier General would come to visit us as they were scouting the area for logistics and in preparation for future military action. One could feel it in the air that intensified military action is in the offing. The Bangladesh Army Officers also started to visit us in increasing number, some along with their wives if they were there; by this time besides Lulu, Tulu and Daliah, there was Khuku *vabi* and a newcomer trained nurse Padda, this made it a nice place for the officers' wives-in-exile to socialize. And of course, Maj. Khaled Mosharraf, (who around this time was promoted to Lt Colonel) would be visiting us almost every other evening, if not every evening. Following brisk visit to the

Confession of a Terrorist!
Chapter 4   Tent Hospital

patients' tents, he would be hanging out with the young ladies in awe, who adored their real-life war hero.

One afternoon around 14:00 or 15:00 Hr., we were extremely busy with a horde of new patients; everyone was doing their best and more to tend to the needs. Naturally, there was no one in the Medical Supplies Tent. We heard and then saw an Indian Army jeep coming to the compound; there was an Officer and our 3rd year medical student Zubayer. While the Officer came to see our activity in the patient tent, Zubayer did not accompany him. Recalling Zubayer's habit of giving away medicine to the Freedom Fighters, I intimated Capt. Akhtar's Batman Taher about my inkling. It seemed that he too had the same suspicion; unbeknown to me apparently Zubayer had interloped into the Medical Supply Tent a few times before. Taher left the patient he was tending to, took his submachine gun, cocked it and went to the Medical Supply Tent. There he caught Zubayer red-hand stealing the medicine that we acquired with so much toil. Taher pointed the gun at him, roared "Hands Up" and escorted him out; the Indian Army Officer was much too embarrassed to say anything; he left with Zubayer in a hurry as Zubayer was a 'medical officer' in the Awami League-affiliated *Mukti Bahini* camp of his.

The "Bloody" Civilians

I had mentioned earlier how I was impressed with my first acquaintance with an Indian Military, rather paramilitary officer, Major Chouhan of the Border Security Force (BSF). Certainly the manner in which the Army Officer who accompanied Zubayer discreetly went away was also impressive for not as much as what he did, rather for what he did not. I, as most of us growing-up and living under the Pakistani military rule and the omnipotent Army have been used to seeing their repugnant abuse of power. I don't know how it was in West Pakistan, but in the East, we "bloody" civilians were treated with no more dignity than the ants in the ground. And that attitude was not restricted to the non-Bengalis; even fellow Bengali members of that military machine were behaving in the same manner; it must have been the doctrine of the Pakistani military. I would be remiss and unfair if I did not mention that I saw remnants of that in some of our *Mukti Bahini* officers though most of them were quickly shedding those bad attitude and behavior. This may have been due to

Confession of a Terrorist!
Chapter 4   Tent Hospital

the fact that a) the young men they are commanding are volunteers, many of whom have the same level of education and social/family stature if not more than they have, or b) being in India and seeing the respectful manner in which the Indian officers behave with their civilian population, they are becoming enlightened, or both. But it was encouraging to see the improvement.

I recall, during one of our trips to Agartala, we went to see a movie and were standing in line to purchase the tickets. There was a long line and an Indian Army Colonel was in line just ahead of me. We chitchatted for a short while to be interrupted by my intense curiosity as to why he was wasting his time standing in line with us civilians. "To buy a ticket for the movie, of course" bemused, he answered. I was perplexed; "but you don't have to stand in line!" I said. He probably realized my mistake and very politely told me that in India, there is no difference between civilians and the military, they all must stand in the same line. What a contrast; how civilized! In Pakistan, there was a separate ticket-window for the military, even for the lowest ranking soldier, so that they could bypass us "bloody civilians." This is the fruit of democracy that we had not tasted for 24 years in Pakistan.

Confession of a Terrorist!
Chapter 4　　　　　Tent Hospital

On the contrary, in Pakistan we were growing up fearing the police and the military. Being in a democratic society for the first time, I could not help but be awed by this delicious fruit of democracy; I supposed this is what an egalitarian society looks like. It's interesting: both Pakistan and India became independent of the British rule the same time save a day earlier or later (officially)! While Indian citizens had enjoyed the benefit of a free and democratic society, for much of that brief history of Pakistan was notorious for not just blatant suppression of human rights and democracy insofar as the majority Bengalis is concerned, but military rule for the entire country.

This was our brief and nascent exposure to a democratic society where people have rights, human rights that is. But bad habits are hard to shed, especially if they are ingrained from your birth. During one of the trips to Agartala our driver Gafoor whom I had introduced before as not the coolest driver in the world hit a pedestrian at the entrance to the town. It was nothing major, not even minor; the pedestrian was lightly hit, rather touched or bumped by the front fender. Incidences like this are common in East Pakistan. The pedestrians are used to such assault from the automobiles – the people who drive or worse own automobiles are richer,

Confession of a Terrorist!
Chapter 4　　　　　Tent Hospital

superior, of higher class etc., etc. So they do not protest; they simply take the abuse unless it is something serious like broken bone or cuts etc. Still not enlightened by the rights of citizens in a democracy, Gafoor decided to ignore and drive on. The gentleman who was hit had obviously expected us to stop. Realizing that it was a hit-and-run, he was shouting at us and started to run in our direction to try to catch us. In no time a band of fellow pedestrians were chasing us shouting "*Mukti Bahini* has hit a man, stop them!" 'Pedal to the metal' with tires screeching Gafoor sped off except it was a crowded area with snarled traffic; fortunately he managed to shake them off. Not only our outfit and demeanor was strikingly different than the local fellow Bengalis, but in contrast to most of the vehicles, ours was also out of the ordinary – a blue Toyota made in Japan [India had indigenously produced Ambassador cars that were less ostentatious and hence not as conspicuous]. We were afraid that we might not be that lucky during our return trip as that was the only way out of town to *Darogar Tilla*. So we waited and waited; we went shopping and window shopping to kill time. Agartala is not a big city, at least not then; so there was not a whole lot one could do. After dusk we decided to give it a try. Thank goodness, we made it safe without any incidence; that is there in Agartala.

Confession of a Terrorist!
Chapter 4   Tent Hospital

Relieved that we were not manhandled, we were singing on our way back. It was a moonlit night, full moon or pretty close. This is a less-traveled road, even more so at night. The road careened around and in between hills and hillocks. To enjoy the moonlight to the fullest someone, I think it was Capt. Akhtar who suggested that Gafoor should turn the headlights off, and so he did. We were having fun; then all of a sudden, boom!

The van started to go zigzag and somewhat out of control. Fortunately we were not going fast. Gafoor had managed to take control and bring it to a stop without any untoward harm to the car or us. We had a flat tire that needed to be replaced. The rest of our return trip was uneventful.

CHAPTER 5

BAMBOO HOSPITAL

gain it was exactly a month later, on 26th August 1971 that we moved from our Tent Hospital to this newly constructed hospital complex. We are in for a treat; this is a complex of bamboo structures that is Capt. Akhtar's dream-come-true. One Mr. Habul Banerjee a local businessman, a landowner and a philanthropist had very kindly let part of his *Leechu Bagan* (lychee orchard) in Bisramgonj to be used for the hospital. Himself, a refugee origin-ally from Comilla, back during the 'partition' of India, he could not only empathize

Confession of a Terrorist!
Chapter 5 Bamboo Hospital

with our need and struggle, but was more than happy to do something for his motherland too.

Mr. Habul Banerjee (third from left) with the hospital staff
Photo courtesy: Dr. A. Q. M. Mahmood (second from left).

The hospital complex was about a couple of hundred meters from the Sonamura-Agartala road, now a highway. As we approached the hospital, ahead and slightly to the left was a pond about 50 m in maximum dimension. The water was rather clear and clean. The hospital complex was to the right; there were two main rectangular houses, reminiscent of the typical school houses in rural Bangladesh with two rows of beds along the length; everything - the pillars, the walls, much of the roof, the beds for the patients as well as those for us,

Confession of a Terrorist!
Chapter 5   Bamboo Hospital

the work-tables, all were made of bamboo. For additional bed capacity steel beds were brought in. The total patient bed-capacity was about a hundred. Then there was an Emergency room, operating room, accommodation for everyone depending on the rank and gender; a large dormitory also made of bamboo was for the females, which was all the way to the north end. The living quarters for the staff other than the doctors and nurses had three-tier bunk-beds, also made of bamboo. You can see the interior of the staff housing in the accompanying pictures.

View of Bangladesh Hospital complex from Bisramgonj-Agartala Road. Photo courtesy: Dr. A. Q. M. Mahmood.

My living accommodation was immediately adjacent to the main hospital building, however in a tent; but compared to that in *Darogar Tilla* this one was different. One has to walk down a couple

Confession of a Terrorist!
Chapter 5   Bamboo Hospital

of steps to enter the tent; the floor was about a meter below the ground level, so the tent was not obstructing the view or otherwise an eyesore. In this 3x3 m tent there were 4 beds made of bamboo. That means I did not have to sleep on the *hogla* mat on the earthen floor. In the beginning, Sq. Ldr. Sadruddin was sharing the tent with me.

Within a few days after we had moved, a large group of Freedom Fighters came back. Alam brought his two sisters Asma and Reshma with

Another view of the Bangladesh Hospital: Note the flagpole in the foreground. The national flag of the Peoples' Republic of Bangladesh was hoisted and taken down every day with full military honor. Photo courtesy: Dr. A. Q. M. Mahmood.

Confession of a Terrorist!
Chapter 5   Bamboo Hospital

him; and to my eternal gratitude and happiness brought me the voluminous Cecil & Loeb's Text Book of Medicine that I requested him. One of my best friends, Farooq Mahmood also came with him and so were Minu Billah, Zakia Hussein *et al.* Of course, Mahmood became my tent-mate along with Sq. Ldr. Sadruddin. Kiron Shankar Debnath also a medical student - a year junior to us joined soon thereafter and was our tent-mate. Kiron's sister Anupoma also a University of Dhaka student joined us a few days later to provide nursing care to our wounded and sick Freedom Fighters.

Kiron used to play guitar in his spare time and was quite good at it; he still does. But unlike Gopi Kashem in Melaghor and Sonamura, Kiron did not entertain us or even himself with his guitar. I don't recall whether he had brought it with him or not. Even if he did, he hardly had any time to play. Perhaps he was much stronger mentally. Or, maybe he did not have the need to cope with the situation as Kashem; after all unlike Kashem, Kiron was not going inside the occupied Bangladesh again and face danger in combat operations. But this line of reasoning should not belittle Kiron's plight either; as a Hindu, he was persecuted by the Pakistani military and that's no little trauma. As a matter of fact, he fled from his dormitory at the

Confession of a Terrorist!
Chapter 5   **Bamboo Hospital**

Dhaka Medical College and left with his meager belongings to cross the border to India. He was running for his life; guitar was the last thing in his mind! Kiron played guitar well though, it would have been a welcome respite to listen.

"Sir, my raiding party is leaving for Bangladesh tonight...

In here, as in *Darogar Tilla*, with increased bed-capacity, we had increased number of patients. There were two major wards – a Medical and a Surgical, but no Obstetrics & Gynecological wards perhaps because there were no female Freedom Fighters in active combat!

The varieties of ailments were similar as before, malaria, diarrhea, dysentery, combat injuries with bullet wounds, deep and rugged cuts from shrapnel etc. Because of the epidemic nature of diarrhea, we would get those patients in volumes – 15 to 20 at a time; that had put a lot of pressure on me at the beginning, at least till Dr. Nazim, Mahmood and Kiron arrived. Almost like a routine, we had a batch of diarrhea patients; again these boys were aged between 15 and 18; some of them were perhaps younger but they were hiding or falsifying

Confession of a Terrorist!
Chapter 5   Bamboo Hospital

Interior of the Hospital made of bamboo, showing patients with combat injuries. Sacs of stones attached to the patients' lower limb with ropes served as improvised traction device for management of fractures. Kiron (extreme left) and a medical assistant Alim (center) are treating in the rear; Mahmood with eyeglasses and black sweater is in the foreground. Photo courtesy: Dr. A. Q. M. Mahmood.

their true age for fear that they won't be allowed to join the *Mukti Bahini*.

Confession of a Terrorist!
Chapter 5   Bamboo Hospital

The diarrhea that these young boys suffered from was intractable; they would be so dehydrated and weak that they could hardly get up from bed. Furthermore, they would come only at the last moment being moribund in case they miss the opportunity to go inside Bangladesh for their missions! Thanks to my self-education and adaptation of the American-medicine, courtesy of Cecil & Loeb, and the antibiotics from the Missionaries, my patients would be on their way to recovery after about 24-48 hours; that is to say, they would not have the diarrhea any longer, but still too weak to even talk!

One 15-year old came from Nirvoypur the night before, and the following morning when I went to visit him, he gave me a look as if nothing had happened to him. I was delighted to see him recover, but he needed at least a couple of days of bedrest and hyperalimentation before I could discharge him. When I asked him how he was doing he replied without answering my question: *"**Sir, my raiding party is leaving for Bangladesh tonight; can you fix me up so that I can go with them to kill some Pakis**?"*

Confession of a Terrorist!
Chapter 5   Bamboo Hospital

Another view of the interior of Bangladesh Hospital made almost exclusively of bamboo, in Bisramgonj showing patients with combat injuries in legs, arms, chest etc. Photo courtesy: Dr. A. Q. M. Mahmood.

Now, going inside Bangladesh to carry out guerilla operations is no easy task. The inductees will have to carry their own weapons, explosives, hand-grenades etc. and trek for hours to cover 20-30 km. Here is a kid who could not even get up from his bed much less lift a 0.303 rifle; and all he wanted is to go on a raid to kill the enemy! I tried to convince him that I would do my best, but that

Confession of a Terrorist!
Chapter 5   Bamboo Hospital

he would have to wait for the next raiding party. He was so very disappointed. But he was not the only one by any means; there were others who would make the same plea. The patients on either side of his bed were intently looking at us with utmost curiosity in their eyes to see what my response was going to be; they decided not to try, at least not that morning. But one was persistent, his reasoning: he came a day earlier than the one I refused to let go!

Another kid; this one hardly 14, came from Shaldanadi Sub-Sector (Capt. Salek, Commanding Officer) riddled by 7 bullets! He was a nascent recruit who had just completed his training and was on his first assignment in a bunker facing the Pakistan army position not more than 500 m across. After being holed-up overnight on his first night in the bunker, early in the morning he wanted to get a breath of fresh air outside; he got out and started to stretch his body. Dot...dot...dot...dot...dot...dot...dot... sounded the machine gun from the Pakistan army position and came the barrage of bullets. By 08:30 or 09:00 Hr. he was in the hospital. All in all, he had taken 7 bullets with an entry and exit wound for each of them, i.e. he had 14 bullet-holes in his body! Fortunately, none of the bullets hit any vital areas or organs,

Confession of a Terrorist!
Chapter 5   Bamboo Hospital

and none remained. In other words, all of the bullets had passed through, most of them in his legs and thighs; there was one in his belly that too went through the skin and came out! After I had taken care of his wounds he immediately got up and wanted to go back to the front with his buddies who brought him to the hospital! He wanted to go back to fight the Pakistani military who had made his tender youthful body into a sieve! He did not stay in the hospital and left for Saldanadi soon thereafter. What examples of fierce determination and patriotism!

That this young man came from Saldanadi Sub-Sector tempted me to visit the area; its commander Capt. Salek was also a classmate of mine at the Notre Dame College, Dhaka (1963-1965). I was also told that my Dhaka Medical College classmate Ali Hafiz Selim was the medical officer there and that they are operating in and from Bangladesh territory and not from India. All of these were very alluring. So, a day or two later quite coincidentally when there was a relative quiet-period in the hospital, Ali Hafiz Selim came to pick me up to visit his area.

We drove about 10 km towards Agartala, and around Bishalgar made a left turn going west towards

Confession of a Terrorist!
Chapter 5 Bamboo Hospital

the Bangladesh border, continued on for another 7-8 km, left our jeep in India and started to walk through the rice fields. We walked for nearly 2 km or so; suddenly a pleasant breeze swept across my face. It was soothing and very refreshing; I felt as if all my fatigue has just vanished with that gust. To confirm my suspicion, curiously I asked Selim how far the border to Bangladesh was; "we are crossing it now; do you smell the air?" he replied with a smile as though he had anticipated my question. I never felt anything like that before; or maybe I had but never appreciated it. Obviously Selim (who several years later died in a tragic auto accident in Libya) have had the pleasure of enjoying it all the time; he told me that every time he crosses this strip of land, he can feel the difference in the air!

I spent the night in the Sub-Sector Head-Quarter only a kilometer or so from our Bangladesh Army positions. The next morning, I asked Capt. Salek as to the location where the Pakistan army made a sifter out of the body of the 14-year old Freedom Fighter. He showed me the Pakistan Army bunkers from a distance but would not take me up close lest I take the enemy fire; for he could not afford to lose his friend, and perhaps as importantly if not more, a 'medicine-man'.

Confession of a Terrorist!
Chapter 5   Bamboo Hospital

Standing in the foreground from left to right: Kiron (red checkered shirt), Mahmood, Professor Bishnu Kanta Bharati (The Editor of *Dharmayug*), Dr. Mobin talking to an unidentified member of *Dharmayug* team (attaché in hand), Dr. Nazim and myself. The bamboo wall of the hospital reception area is in the background. Photo credit: *Dharmayug,* courtesy Dr. A. Q. M. Mahmood.

Where is the Beef?!

If I was remiss in clarifying, most of our patients in Bisramgonj had combat wounds. It appeared to me that despite all the proper medicine and care, their wounds were not healing at the rate I expected, much less theirs; they wanted the wounds to heal instantly like a fast-forwarded

Confession of a Terrorist!
Chapter 5   Bamboo Hospital

cinematography, so that they could go back and kill more Pakistani soldiers! I suspected that they may be suffering from protein malnourishment; after all, they were getting meat once a week, and even then it was hardly any more than 20-30 gm! Goat-meat (mutton) was the only source of meat in a place where cattle enjoy a godly status.

I decided to go for shopping for a cow; in Tripura, a conservative mostly Hindu society that's a suicidal mission. But our boys needed protein and that's the best we could do. Gafoor our driver and I went to Melaghor Bazaar, about 8 km or so along with Taher (this was a day or two before he fell ill). As soon as we arrived in the Bazaar, there was not just a palpable, but almost an audible hum; "*Mukti Bahini* is here for the [sacred] cows!" To offset that I asked Taher, who is extremely street-smart to look for a milking cow; and to spread the word around that our wounded Freedom Fighters need milk for their nourishment. Like dousing wildfire, it worked like a charm! The market place was quieter.

With the attention of the shoppers now on Taher the unmistakable and instantly noticeable *Mukti Bahini* and Gafoor, no one was paying attention to me, who as you can see from the picture, is as

Confession of a Terrorist!
Chapter 5   Bamboo Hospital

emaciated as a man in his dying days. I had my eyes on a cow that looked very healthy and negotiated a reasonable price. I had asked Gafoor to bring the pickup truck up close; paid for the cow, immediately put it on the back of the truck and asked Gafoor to move; all in less than 60 seconds!

Gafoor, as I had mentioned before was not the coolest driver; he put the 'pedal to the metal' and to our horror made screeching sound of the wheels. As he sped off in panic, the acceleration was so fast that the cow fell off the truck! Holy cow!! It didn't take more than a second for the crowd to realize what was going on: "*Mukti Bahini* was taking the cow to the camp to slaughter" was the chant... A wild mob was chasing us. I was in the back of the truck with Taher and the cow. Taher and I instantly got off on the street and picked up the cow. Now, this is not a big Black Angus 500+ kg cow, but it was no lamb either; it was an average Indian cow – at least 200 kg if not more. Again I don't know how just the two of us, Taher and I picked up this whole cow who was putting up its own fight to let loose, from the street, lifted it up 0.5 meter in the back of the pickup truck; thanks to adrenaline I guess, we closed the rear gate of the truck, I pushed Gafoor from the dri-

Confession of a Terrorist!
Chapter 5   Bamboo Hospital

ver's seat, took control and sped off, this time without the hazard of leaving the cow behind and being attacked by an angry mob all in 3-4 seconds, tops. You may recall that this was not the first time we were being chased by an angry mob; that was in the outskirts of Agartala. But the stakes are much higher here; our hospital is not far from this place and we frequently travel this road.

Within an hour of our arrival at the hospital, the cow was slaughtered, cooked and the patients had a feast. For most, this was the first taste of beef in months. We disposed-off any and all incriminating evidence of slaughtering a cow considered sacred in an ultraconservative part of India, within an hour.

As malnourished and deprived as our boys were, they certainly were not lacking in their magnanimity and gratitude. We would try to finish our treatment and assessment 'rounds' outside their mealtime, except for emergency situations. Mahmood told me that on occasions when he happened to be present during their mealtime our Freedom Fighters would offer him their meager rations as sign of gratefulness and camaraderie.

Confession of a Terrorist!
Chapter 5   Bamboo Hospital

Ethical Dilemma

Taher, Capt. Akhtar's Batman fell ill one day. Apparently he became fond of me. Though his sole personal responsibility and loyalty was to Capt. Akhtar, to my mild embarrassment, he would offer his services to me as well. I would be less than honest if I stated that I did not take him up on that; it felt privileged to be pampered. During this epidemic, no matter how small or contained it was, Taher came down with intractable diarrhea. Taher was a very strong man with rather imposing physique for an average Bengali, for his figure was anything but average Bengali - about 181cm, 80+ kg and very well-built. Within 48 hours he was beginning to look like me! His belly became hollowed in, eyes sunken and cheeks retracted; his ribs became prominent as the muscles in between rapidly wasted, one could count his ribs from a distance. Taher did not want to take-up a hospital bed for himself; he wanted that to be available for the combat wounded Freedom Fighters; he preferred to stay in his staff quarter. On the other hand, that means he had the privilege of getting personalized care and house call! But we had to get a special extra patient-bed for him as the bamboo bunk beds would not allow

Confession of a Terrorist!
Chapter 5   Bamboo Hospital

us to manage him promptly and efficiently in the unlikely event of an emergency.

Dr. Nazim came from Melaghor Head-Quarter clinic to the Bisramgonj hospital and by now he was taking full load of work if not more. As Taher checked-in, he took care of him; so technically and for all purposes that matter, Taher was 'his patient.' It did not go unnoticed to Taher that my patients with similar condition were begging me to go back to the front or inside the enemy-occupied Bangladesh for operations within 24 hours of initiation of their treatment. So, when after 2-3 days he was not ready to get off the bed except for the toilet every 2-3 hours he asked me whether I could help him. Sadly, I had to tell him that ethically I could not, as he was Dr. Nazim's patient and unless Dr. Nazim asked me or relinquished him to me, or he requested Dr. Nazim to transfer him to me (an idea he did not think was politically sound, lest Dr. Nazim takes offense) I would be unable to comply. Needless to say, Taher did not expect that answer and was disappointed. Then came a lucky break; Dr. Nazim had to go to Agartala on some urgent business for the day and wanted me to take care of his patients, one of whom was Taher.

Confession of a Terrorist!
Chapter 5   Bamboo Hospital

Yahoo! After seeing my patients, the first of Dr. Nazim's I went to see was Taher. He was dehydrated and I essentially pumped him with a lot of intravenous fluids, the antibiotics that I got from my Missionary friends and anything else. By late that afternoon, Taher did not have to go to the toilet anymore, and the next day he was walking about.

As you can see from the picture of him and me, as sick as he was, he looked much healthier than his doctor (!); that tells you what a great physique he had. That afternoon, he feasted on the beef that he, Gafoor and I bought from Melaghor market with the crowd hounding after us. "It was the most delicious meat" he exclaimed at the first bite of solid-food after his 96+ hours of ordeal with diarrhea.

While the tent hospital in *Darogar Tilla* became a popular showcase for politicians and dignitaries, the bamboo hospital was even more, a lot more. We had streams of visitors; I started to worry if it would distract the staff from patientcare responsibilities. But it was also necessary for a variety of reasons, not least of which was public relations to boost the morale of our people both inside and outside the Pakistan-occupied Bangladesh.

Confession of a Terrorist!
Chapter 5   Bamboo Hospital

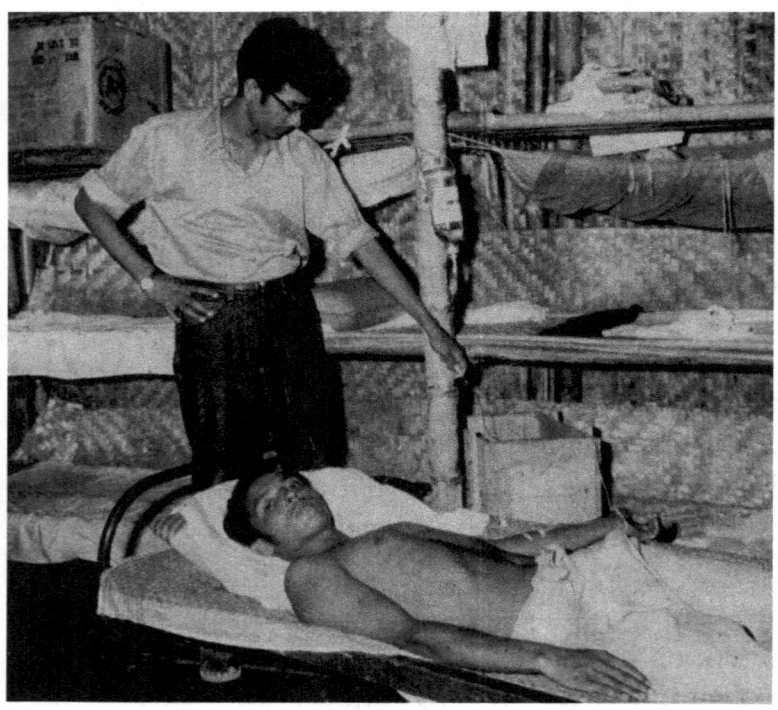

My first opportunity to treat Taher with grim face, sunken eyeballs and abdomen, and ribcage showing emaciation. Photo credit: *Dharmayug,* courtesy Dr. A. Q. M. Mahmood.

While Taher was under my care, we received several patients with combat injury; Kiron, Mahmood and I rushed to meet them at the entrance for triage. In an amazing feat of coincidence, when we were walking back to the Emergency Room, a reporter and photographer from the Indian monthly magazine *Dharmayug* came over and started shooting pictures. They were very

Chapter 5   Bamboo Hospital

impressed by the hospital and were touched by the morale, determination and patriotism of our fine boys and girls. A very nice article with several pictures came out in the 14 November 1971 issue of the magazine; the pictures are reproduced from a copy of the magazine; Farooq Mahmood happened to have the only copy available; he had kindly lent me for the book. Thank goodness for these pictures and the article, we have some documentary evidence saved for posterity.

The Nursing Staff

Except for Podda (also spelled as Padma) who was presumably a trained nurse or nurse-in-training, the rest of the brave women volunteers who gave our Freedom Fighters much needed nursing care were University of Dhaka students.

With the arrival of additional students - Asma, Reshma, Minu Billah, and a lecturer at Eden College, Dhaka - Zakia Hussein and others, there were plenty of people to give our Freedom Fighters tender loving nursing care. And care for our Freedom Fighters was not all they did. They carried out a lot of other ancillary activities not directly related to patient care. Daliah to my gratitude willingly did not only do my laundry but also that of my

Confession of a Terrorist!
Chapter 5   Bamboo Hospital

friend Mahmood's; a fact he still fondly recalls with gratitude.

Mahmood (left with glasses) and Kiron (red shirt) and I (blue shirt rear and far right with glasses) are accompanying a combat-wounded Freedom Fighter as he is being brought in. The patient's suffering is evident as he was tossing and turning on the stretcher. The men carrying the stretcher are cooks who also work in other capacity such as this as necessary. Photo credit: *Dharmayug,* courtesy Dr. A. Q. M. Mahmood.

These beautiful women also were an added attraction to our Sector Commander Khaled Mosharraf who appeared to be spending more and more time at the hospital, not with the patients but with the

Confession of a Terrorist!
Chapter 5   Bamboo Hospital

young ladies. And they loved it; they got to be with a real-life war hero who happened to have the charm and looks of a movie-star. I noted back in Sonamura that Daliah became infatuated with him. Leaving everything aside she would rush to be in his company as soon as there was indication of his presence. She would be animated just by being in his company, did not matter that there were others too! She would be fidgeting without herself knowing it. There in Sonamura at the Rest House Hospital, Maj. Khaled had expressed his dissatisfaction with his senior commanders and the Commander-in-Chief; I was disturbed by the tone and content of those musing as they were suggestive of mutiny in the brew. We don't even have a country realistically speaking. Here in the infancy of this Liberation War we are outside the country fighting for our independence with meager force, that too courtesy of our Indian friends who could in theory cut off the supply and other support at any moment, and he is thinking of mutiny!

From the way Daliah reacted when I shared my discontent and apprehension about this, I realized that she was madly in love with the war-hero. At Bisramgonj, as I had hardly any spare time left, Daliah and I were drifting apart, a vacuum conve-

Confession of a Terrorist!
Chapter 5   Bamboo Hospital

niently filled by Lt Col Khaled Mosharraf. I was perplexed and heartbroken. Was she doing my laundry as a token of her love or just doing her duty as a part of serving her country as she wash-

Some of the young ladies who volunteered nursing care at the Bangladesh Hospital are seated in front of their dormitory in their leisure time. While they never participated in military operations, one or two had expressed their desire to Lt Col Khaled Mosharraf to do so. Photo credit: *Dharmayug,* courtesy Dr. A. Q. M. Mahmood.

ed my friend Mahmood's clothes too. So, did she really love me or was it just an illusion? Retrospectively on the other hand, as emaciated and

Confession of a Terrorist!
Chapter 5 Bamboo Hospital

unattractive as I became, Lt Col Khaled Mosharraf was certainly a better choice!

Sq. Ldr. Sadruddin was a keen observant person. It seems that whenever there is more than one person, there is politics. Both Sq. Ldr. Sadruddin and I noted that the girls were also becoming polarized into groups, some hating the guts of others. The city girls were looking down on the ones from the small towns and villages and so. There were petty girlish fights; Daliah used to complain that certain other girls were picking on her. Could it be possible that there were jealousy that Lt Col Khaled Mosharraf liked her over others? Did they sense that the two were in love? Lt Col Khaled Mosharraf's daily visits in the evening and spending an inordinate amount of time with the ladies did not evade Sq. Ldr. Sadruddin's eyes either. Feeling my obvious unhappiness, he started to renew his enticement for me to go to his Sub-Sector in Dinajpur. I don't think that my happiness was the only reason he was tempting me to go there; he needed someone in his Sub-Sector and realized that owing to my personal state of affairs I would now be more willing to comply; what a strategist! A few days after our move to the Bamboo Hospital in Bisramgonj he went back to his Sub-Sector and left me his contact information; under the circumstances, I told him that I certainly was planning to leave this sector (Sector 2); I may either go to my high school buddy Flt Lt Nurul Kader's Sub-Sector in Sector 4 (Col C. R. Datta Commanding) or to his, in Sector 6.

Engineer Nazrul Islam

It was a rainy night. At around 21:00 Hr. we received a busload of young Freedom Fighters all with either intractable diarrhea or malaria. There seemed to be an epidemic of both. There must have been over 20 patients. I was just about the only physician treating them. Dr. Nazim, the only other physician was away and so was Capt. Akhtar. I had to start intravenous infusion of saline for all of the diarrhea patients; the "nurses" except for Podda may be, were not really qualified to do that. As you can imagine it was chaotic. At the same time came a middle-aged gentleman, Engineer Nazrul Islam. He had been staying at the Head-Quarter in Melaghor and developed very high fever, shaking chills, was confused and rambling. I realized that this was no regular malaria; he had cerebral malaria that carries a near 100% rate of mortality. There, at least at that time and place, the only treatment I could give was intramuscular

Chapter 5   Bamboo Hospital

chloroquine; as per the best of my knowledge that would offer some chance of success. But, time is of the essence; we may not succeed if the medicine is received too late in the disease process. Having given him the treatment and instructions to the nursing staff for further treatment schedules, I continued to work on the other Freedom Fighters who too needed my urgent attention just as badly. It must have been past midnight that I was finally done and retired to my bed in the tent closest to the Medical Unit of the hospital.

The next morning I was awakened with a wail; a patient had died; our first casualty in three months or so. I immediately realized that it must be Engineer Nazrul Islam, and it was. Not that he had any chance, but still I felt very miserable by the fact that I could not save him. Alas! Nothing I did or anybody could do, could have saved him; that is the 'nature of the beast' called cerebral malaria; neither the American-type of treatment from Cecil & Loeb, nor the highest quality of medicine from UK and Australia that I procured from the Missionaries kept him alive.

After the body was removed there was some insinuation that he died due to drug reaction. I am not sure who the author of that misinformation/disin-

Confession of a Terrorist!
Chapter 5   Bamboo Hospital

formation was. Engineer Nazrul Islam was the brother-in-law of a Member of the Parliament in exile and relative of two other members of the *Mukti Bahini* including the 3rd year medical student Zubayer. Be that as it may, Dr. M. A. Mobin an orthopedic surgeon felt that he needed to supervise me henceforth.

Drs. Mobin and Zafrullah Chowdhury had lived and trained in UK since the mid to late 1960's. I only met Dr. Zafrullah once or may be twice when he was visiting us at the bamboo hospital, subsequently called Bangladesh Hospital in Bisramgonj or Bisramgonj Bangladesh Hospital. I knew of Dr. Zafrullah as not only he was a well-known student leader at Dhaka Medical College, but he was also the elder brother of a classmate of mine also at Notre Dame College (1963-1965). In the early 1960's there was a 'student movement' in Dhaka Medical College that disgustingly resulted in the assault of Dr. Asiruddin, the then Professor of Surgery. It was then that Dr. Zafrullah was active as a student leader (General Secretary of the Students' Union) and was involved in the 'student movement.' Following this "turbulent student life, he finished his MBBS degree in 1964 and left for UK for postgraduate studies" in surgery.[1] I was

---

[1] http://en.wikipedia.org/wiki/Zafrullah_Chowdhury

Confession of a Terrorist!
Chapter 5   Bamboo Hospital

not sure if he had completed his required training and received the coveted F̲ellow of the R̲oyal C̲ollege of S̲urgery (FRCS) degree during those seven years that he was in UK. Anyway, being in politics from his Medical-student-days, he apparently was busy and perhaps more comfortable with the politicians of the government-in-exile in Kolkata. I understood that he was instrumental in organizing the Bamboo Hospital we're using now.

Dr. Mobin on the other hand was intimately involved with the construction of the hospital; he worked tirelessly to supervise it day and night and made sure that it had all the necessary structural organization for a modern facility, albeit primitively made solely of bamboo. It was not clear whether Dr. Mobin too had the recognized FRCS degree and was a Consultant Orthopedic Surgeon there in UK.

The treatment regimens for many diseases vary from country to country. My methods of treatment as per the authoritative United States text book Cecil & Loeb were quite different from those in UK text books of medicine, mostly insofar as dosage is concerned. Thus, much of my treatment regimen may have been unfamiliar to Dr. Mobin. He being several years senior to me, and more importantly a founder of the hospital itself and UK-trained, felt that I needed to be closely supervised to the point that he was questioning every single of my patient management protocols and prescriptions. Aside from demoralizing me, I found this behavior and attitude quite undignified and intrusive; in protest, I would tell him that if he thought I was wrong and hence incompetent, then he should take over the patients' care; with that I would immediately relinquish the responsibility of the case to him. After 2-3 such incidents, he backed off and let me treat my patients the way I wanted to.

Crime & Punishment/Banishment

I felt that being in this large hospital in a secure area outside the range of Pakistani army artillery range was not how I would have liked to serve the Freedom Fighters ideally; before I left Dhaka I dreamt of serving them at the battlefront where the action is, so that I could be attending to them without delay, as in some cases delays of a few minutes could cost the life. Besides, it seemed heroic! I therefore had requested Capt. Akhtar and Lt Col Khaled Mosharraf several times that I be sent to the Sub-Sectors where our *Mukti Bahini* fighters are fighting the enemy; my plea fell on

Confession of a Terrorist!
Chapter 5 Bamboo Hospital

deaf ears; I was most needed at the hospital here, was the answer like a broken record. Now, a few days after the heartbreaking demise of Engineer Nazrul Islam, the same Lt Col Mosharraf who appeared concerned (?!) for my safety in Sonamura for risking my life in raiding Pakistan army position, wanted to transfer me to Belonia, a Sub-Sector farthest from the hospital in the entire Sector 2! This seemed like a convenient excuse to send me away: a patient dies under my care; I could not help but wonder whether the fact that he was flirting with my beloved Daliah and that she was madly in love with him had anything to do with my planned banishment from the hospital to the outermost corner of the Sector!

These events made me more and more resolute in my decision to leave the Sector. And Sq. Ldr. Sadruddin's offer was looking more and more attractive by the minute. My first choice however was to go to Flt Lt Nurul Kader in Sector 4. I tried to contact him many times in vain; his Sub-Sector is in a very inaccessible area deep in the jungles of Assam, denser than those in Tripura. Reluctantly, I had decided to go to Sector 6.

Fortunately, that was also the last, and the only patient I had lost. The aftermath of that however

Confession of a Terrorist!
Chapter 5   Bamboo Hospital

continued past the liberation of the country. I was being hunted, but [luckily] in the wrong place. I came to know that, with submachine guns in their hands and ammunition belts on the shoulder, some still-distraught freedom fighter relatives of Engineer Nazrul Islam – the avengers were looking for me at Daliah's parents' house [thank goodness they did not know my parent's house!]. And that was not the end of it either; a couple of days later, in a neighborhood clubhouse in Gopibag they were planning how to take 'revenge' on me; this time Capt. Akhtar happened to be present. Realizing their motive, he tried to convince them that the death[2] of Engineer Nazrul Islam was for no fault of mine and heaped praises on me in vain. Sensing that they were unimpressed and undeterred, he stood up and pulled out his service pistol and challenged anyone to harm me, for they would have to confront him first before they could think of killing me! I suppose that did it. A million thanks to Major Dr. Akhtar Ahmed, I am still alive today! I owe him my life.

---

[2] A road in Tikatuli-Haatkhola area in Dhaka has been renamed as "*Shaheed* Nazrul Islam Avenue" which is presumably to honor Engineer Nazrul Islam. As per the Webster's Dictionary a martyr (*Shaheed*) "is a person who willingly suffers death rather than renounces his or her religion or a person who is put to death or suffers on behalf of a cause." One is left to wonder whether the numerous "*Shaheeds*" whose names are now everywhere in Bangladesh are true martyrs or not.

Confession of a Terrorist!
Chapter 5   Bamboo Hospital

With these events affecting me personally, the last few days were demoralizing. I could not help but feel apathetic although I tried my very best for that not to be reflected on my patient care. Around this time, besides others, came a senior medical student - Morshed and Capt. Dr. Sitara Begum. Capt. Sitara was two years senior to me in Dhaka Medical College. She had joined the Pakistan Military as a Medical Officer like Capt. Dr. Akhtar, and now has joined us. Evidently, patriotism and bravery runs in her family; she is the sister of Capt. Haider - the Special Forces officer in Melaghor. Aside from her and the other brave girls working in the hospital, our history is rather rich insofar as the role of women in our resistance is concerned; Pritilata Waddedar, Moharani Lakshmi Bai - the Queen of Jhasi are two of the notable female firebrand patriots and freedom fighters from the past.

CHAPTER 6

TARGET 6

Certainly I was disgusted with my personal situation in Bisramgonj and was preparing to go to Sector 6 leaving my sweet Daliah with the love of her life. For her own interest, obviously, she tried to convince me to stay, to no avail. Seeing my determination, she started crying which did not persuade me either. When on 27th June we left Dhaka to come to Tripura, Daliah's mother had entrusted me with her safety and life; someone inside me, conscience I suppose, was telling that I must honor that pledge no matter what the price was going to be. Thus, most reluctantly I had con-

Confession of a Terrorist!
Chapter 6   Target 6

sented to her accompanying me; and price I paid very dearly.

Daliah's younger brother Shelley had left with Ulfat (the first terrorist I met who gave me the earliest credible information about *Mukti Bahini* and the need for medical help) and another of his friend Manzoor (younger brother of Capt. Dr. Akhtar Ahmed) back in mid-April presumably to join *Mukti Bahini*. As I found out later, they did not come to Sector 2 in Tripura (Agartala) which was closer to Dhaka. Instead they were heading west to Kolkata. That may have been the smartest move as for sure they could find out in Kolkata as to the existence if any, and the whereabouts of the Resistance. On the other hand, to do that in Tripura would be tantamount of trying to find a 'needle in a haystack'. *En route* they stopped in Saatkhira, Daliah's and Shelly's father's hometown. While both Ulfat and Manzoor proceeded on west to Kolkata to find and join the *Mukti Bahini* immediately, Shelley however stayed behind in Saatkhira with his father [his parents had been separated for a while] and extended family. At some point, he eventually crossed into India, but went to his maternal uncles' home (*Mama Bari*) in Murshidabad, West Bengal and stayed there for a while. Manzoor had undergone training

Confession of a Terrorist!
Chapter 6 **Target 6**

in an Indian Military College; following graduation he joined the Bangladesh Liberation Army as a commissioned officer. A few days prior to my planned departure, Shelley suddenly showed up in the hospital; he had recently joined an Awami League operated training camp in Sector 2. He too wanted to go with me, leaving behind his "training" and putative "guerilla operations!"

I still wanted to try to go to Flt. Lt. Nurul Kader's Sub-Sector and work there. For that I needed to go to Shilchar (or Silchar). In mid-October I went to the Indian Airlines office in Agartala to purchase the tickets. In those days without electronic reservation systems, mobile phones etc., one had to reconfirm the reservation either in person or by phone. Since we did not have a phone in the hospital, I had to travel back to Agartala just to reconfirm the reservation. This was not easy as transportation was a problem; we had only that Mazda pickup van. Of course this took me away from the patients I wanted to serve even though I was so demoralized that I could not perform my duties as enthusiastically as I would have liked to. When I went to reconfirm, to my utter surprise and dismay I was told that my reservations were canceled, by the order of Lt Col Khaled Mosharraf. Dejected, I made new reservations for the next available

Confession of a Terrorist!
Chapter 6   Target 6

flight that was convenient for me and returned to the hospital. The same thing happened again; as I went to reconfirm I was told about the cancellation; and I rebooked, again.

The following day after my return to the hospital, around 12:00-13:00 Hr. Lt Col Khaled came to the hospital. That is not his usual evening rendezvous with the ladies, especially Daliah; surprisingly, he came to the patients' ward while I was tending to their needs. As usual he had his service pistol on his holster; but his bodyguard with a sub-machine gun in hand (and not hanging from the shoulder) was also with him. I had decided that I will confront him. Seeing the fury in my face, he wanted to appease me first by saying how much he needed me there [of course!] and said that I did not have to go to Belonia Sub-Sector etc. I, on the other hand charged him for his unauthorized and improper cancellation of my airline reservations. He told me that I was under his command and I had to follow his dictum; to that I replied sternly that I was not one of his military personnel; I was a civilian who joined the *Mukti Bahini* voluntarily; I had joined the Resistance on my free will and I was leaving on my free will as well; he had no authority to stop me – a volunteer. His gun-ready body guard was taken aback by this forceful manner and no-nonsense attitude of mine. I did not think that he was going to shoot me in the hospital unless I did something stupid like physically attacking the Commander, which I would not have done any-way. Capt. Akhtar was also in attendance and was watching the drama with some amusement and a bit of pride for me [his protégé has learnt to fight for himself, I guess was his contentment!]. Lt Col Khaled decided not to pursue the matter anymore [guilt conscience?!] and left saying something like "OK" or "so be it." As soon as he left, Capt. Akhtar instructed me to "always keep your head up; *never* lower it down for anyone" a principle that had become an integral part of my persona ever since. For that too I am ever so grateful to him.

Realizing that this time I would be leaving unimpeded, Taher became very emotional; Capt. Akhtar pretended that he wasn't, but he also had difficulty hiding it. To say that Mahmood was sad is an understatement. I was one of his closest friends; we have been that way since Notre Dame College beginning 1963 and through the Dhaka Medical College days. During the period from 7th March the day Sheikh Mujibur Rahman gave his famous speech, till the early evening of 25 March we were inseparable. We were analyzing the political

Confession of a Terrorist!
Chapter 6   **Target 6**

situations in the country and brainstorming what's in store for the future. All of the scenarios we played were bleak. On the afternoon of 25th March, Mahmood and I went to the Bangla Academy at the University of Dhaka campus to attend a seminar on the political situation of the day and to assess the political mood of the intelligentsia. Strongly sensing imminent catastrophe, we walked to the Engineers' Institute across the Ramna Race Course (currently *Suhrawardi udyan* [garden]) about a kilometer, at dusk. There used to be some peddlers who would sell snacks; we had some *Fuchka*[1] and said 'final' goodbye to each other for we did not know if we shall ever meet again in this life. Thus, for him to see me leave only a few weeks after his joining the *Mukti Bahini* here in India was devastating. We survived one 'final' goodbye; he probably didn't want to say another 'final' goodbye for we might not be so lucky this time. Mahmood was not controlling his emotions; he simply displayed none, he just became taciturn.

Taher came to Agartala airport to see us off. We checked in for Shilchar; there was very little luggage, so we hand-carried our meager belongings. But since there was a scale to weigh the checked-

---

[1] Small spheroids of thin crust filled with chick peas and a tangy broth.

Confession of a Terrorist!
Chapter 6   Target 6

in luggage, I decided to weigh myself. I was down by 10 kg, from 58 kg to 48 kg! As I haven't had the luxury of looking at myself in a mirror [there was none!], I had no idea how my physique had transformed during the past 4 months; I was a bit horrified. It was about 27th or 28th of October, exactly two months after we had moved to the Bamboo Hospital and four months since joining the *Mukti Bahini*.

Flying in a DC 3 and Landing on a Football Field

I had another surprise here; this one was more pleasant; we did not have to go through Customs even though we were travelling from the State of Tripura to Shilchar which is in the State of Assam; in Pakistan we had to go through Customs for travelling from the East to the West and *vice versa!* Naturally, we don't have to; we are in the same country! We proceeded to the airplane – an Indian Airlines Mc Donnel Douglas DC 3 Dakota, a vintage aircraft. It was a smooth take-off. Once in the air I could for the first time really appreciate the lush green vegetation of the state of Tripura. While I had been to the jungles of Melaghor and Nirvoypur, I was within it, in between the trees; but now I have a real birds' eye view, literally.

Confession of a Terrorist!
Chapter 6   Target 6

The denseness of the forests makes it impossible to see anything else on the ground but a green carpet below. Now I realized what it means when someone says you can't appreciate the forest by walking between the trees. After a short flight, we were told to fasten our seatbelts; we're ready to land in Kamalpur, a small town very close, about a kilometer or so, to the Bangladesh border in Sylhet district. Incidentally, Kamalpur is also the name my Dad's village though it may more accurately be spelled as *Komolpur* to be phonetically closer. The town of Kamalpur was about 20 km southeast of Sreemongol in Bangladesh.

I was looking for the airport, but could not find any; all I could see out the window was dense jungle. Where were we going to land?! As the plane was descending to a height barely above the tree-tops, I spotted what looked like a football field, but there was no concrete landing strip (runway)! The wheels started to touch the bare ground and the landing as expected was less than smooth, but all-things-considered, perfect. The airport terminal was not any more impressive than the bamboo hospital I just left, except that it had tin roof and about the size of one of our hospital wards. But what was impressive is that there was air-service in a remote place like this.

Confession of a Terrorist!
Chapter 6   Target 6

After a brief stopover we took off again, this time for Shilchar in southern Assam. Shilchar airport was a regular one with concrete runway. The town is a mid-size one, not too dissimilar than Agartala but looked more prosperous, with railway service deep inside the dense jungles of Assam. Most of the people in Shilchar were Bengalis from East Bengal who had originally migrated from Sylhet, following the creation of Pakistan in 1947. I tried one last time to see if I could go to Flt Lt Nurul Kader's Sub-Sector in Karimgonj area, but to no avail. Thus, we walked to the railway station to go to Lumding railway junction in central Assam. Essentially, we would be traveling northeast to Lumding, take another train and go west to Guwahati on to Shiliguri traveling around the northern borders of Sylhet, Mymensingh, Rongpur and Dinajpur (of Bangladesh).

Murphy's Law

The train from Shilchar to Lumding railway junction left around midnight, the track running almost parallel to the Sylhet border for a while. The exhaustion from the day's extreme emotion, excitement and toil put me to sleep immediately. The train was to make only one stop before arriving at Lumding railway junction at midmorning. But

Confession of a Terrorist!
Chapter 6   Target 6

after a couple of hours, I woke up as the train had suddenly stopped and there was some commotion within the car. We were inside this impenetrable jungle between two tunnels in two hills, one in front and the other behind us. Apparently, the saboteurs from Pakistan Special Forces (terrorists?!) had blown off the train track. So, we had to wait till the tracks were repaired in the middle of the densest jungle and hills that I have ever seen. Notwithstanding this harsh terrain, by day break the track was repaired and the train started to move again, albeit very slowly this time as the Engineer was taking extra precaution to visually check the track. The efficiency of the Indian Railway that I saw there and then was puzzling as, while we were in Pakistan, the propaganda we were bombarded was how inferior India was as a country and society!

By the time we arrived at Lumding railway junction, our connecting train to Guwahati (capital of the State of Assam) left long before. So we had to spend the night in Lumding. There was nothing in Lumding besides the fact that it was a railway junction, a track coming from Shilchar connecting to the ones from Guwahati in the west to the one all the way in the northeastern end of India and Nagaland in Dibrugarh. The train would be runni-

Confession of a Terrorist!
Chapter 6   Target 6

ng only once a day. We had no choice but to go to a 'hotel' that was essentially a shack. We all had to sleep in the same room (about 3x3 m or less) with other strangers – fellow travelers who too missed their train like us. Fortunately a separate bed, not much different from the ones we got in our bamboo hospital was available for Daliah; less than 10 Indian Rupees was the rent for the night for all three of us. Everything that could go wrong went wrong; and I was the person to blame for all the mishaps. Back then as a youth when Shelley liked me and still had some unbiased opinions about me, he to my pleasant surprise was empathizing with me. He tried to make light of the matters and was making an effort to convince his sister to be more reasonable. But that hardly stopped the barrage of complaints from her who was becoming hysterical for having to leave the love of her life and not having a luxury accommodation in the middle of the impenetrable jungles of Assam. It was extremely difficult keeping my cool; to my great surprise, I hadn't lost it for a moment.

The next morning we boarded the famous Dibrugarh Express train that went all the way to the West Bengal town of Shiliguri running almost parallel to the northern border of Bangladesh. This train was grossly overcrowded perhaps owing to

Confession of a Terrorist!
Chapter 6   Target 6

the fact that it had to accommodate an extra trainload of previous day's passengers from Shilchar. Not only were there no seats available, but even standing room was almost nonexistent. We were being squished like sardines in a can; that too was my fault! Being an express train it was moving pretty fast, the rail tracks were broad-gauge, considerably wider and sturdier than the one from Shilchar and in East Pakistan. Apparently, being so far inside India also the threat of Pakistani terrorist blowing the train tracks was very little. We arrived in Guwahati in the evening. I heard of Guwahati many times before from some of my distant uncles who used to live there, and owned small businesses. It seemed that migrants from East Bengal like my uncles had control of the local economy, a fact that the indigenous Assamese resented resulting in later unrest and their expulsion. On the bank of the majestic River Brahmaputra, Guwahati looked pretty at night. At Guwahati, many people got off, and finally we could find some seats after standing for several hours.

We were again rolling for another marathon ride for Shiliguri. The train was running all night through and between the hills (larger ones as we are also running close to the foothills of the Himalaya on the north) and dense jungles of Assam. Very

Confession of a Terrorist!
Chapter 6　　　　　　　　Target 6

early in the morning around 05:00 or so, again I was woken up by sudden stoppage of the train. Was this another act of sabotage by the Pakistani terrorists? Having narrowly escaped from one planned train-wreck and with the terror the Pakistan military inflicted in me beginning 25 March and the saboteurs near Shilchar, it was hard not to be panicked, all the other passengers were screaming; my heart was beating, rather thumping as fast and as strongly it could; felt like my heart was going to come out of my chest. That I was nervous is an understatement. This time the train stopped just a few meters short of a bridge straddling between two hills and over a ravine underneath nearly 200 m below us; a large section of the bridge was washed away by the very heavy rainfall throughout the night [my fault again, and not for the last time either!]. Thank goodness, the Engineer spotted the washed-away bridge just in time and saved the whole train with several hundred if not a thousand or so passengers from certain death. This was between Jalpaiguri and Shiliguri. The Indian Rail had arranged for buses to transport us to Shiliguri train station which was about 20-30 km away to the west.

The bus ride was spectacular, very picturesque. The road to Shiliguri was going through the mou-

Confession of a Terrorist!
Chapter 6   Target 6

ntains, the clouds were either below the road or at the level, and I felt like I could just touch it. This is the second time I am traveling through the mountains; the first time was when I had been to the Khyber Pass in the Northwest Frontier province of West Pakistan. That was also quite spectacular, however the terrain was different and so was the beauty. In here the lush green vegetation, the fog and the first rays of the morning sun was dreamlike. The road was winding between the mountains with steep slopes and deep ravines on the mountainside. The magnificence of the scene distracted me from any possible danger of falling into the ravine. It also helped in alleviating the panic; my heartbeats were coming down gradually.

We arrived at the Shiliguri train station around 08:00 or 08:30. We asked around to find out how to go to Tetulia in Dinajpur; no one at the station could tell us. Dejected, we asked for tickets to go to Kolkata as the Bangladesh Embassy was in Kolkata, where I might be able to find out how to proceed to Sector 6. Heavy rainfall during the past 3-4 days had submerged the train track to Kolkata under floodwater midway near Farakkah; no train to Kolkata! Not knowing anyone in Shiliguri and not being able to go to Sector 6 or to Kolkata we decided that we should try to go to Daliah's maternal uncles' home (*Mama Bari*) in Murshidabad by bus. We were in luck, especially me, as for the first time during this trip Daliah was not complaining. The bus was a modern one for long distance travel, nothing we have seen in East Pakistan before, not even during my trip to West Pakistan. It was an air-conditioned luxury coach, with reclining seats which were plush, and made in India by Tata. Without wishing to belabor the issue, again in Pakistan we had been bombarded with the propaganda as to how the standard of living was low in India as compared to Pakistan, that in Pakistan we had the privilege of getting the luxury items from foreign countries in contrast to the homegrown 'inferior' products in India. We boarded the bus early evening, it traveled all night and around 09:00 in the morning suddenly it came to a stop; one of the tires blew off!

The driver and his help fixed the tire and we were off again. We finally came to Bhagobangola in Murshidabad district and then on to the village of Mohammadpur, about 230 km north of Kolkata.

La Forza del Destino

Here we met Daliah's uncles and cousins. I did not come to India to have fun; I came to aid my

Confession of a Terrorist!
Chapter 6   Target 6

brothers fighting the enemy. My being in Murshidabad district and later in the towns of Murshidabad, Baharampur and Bhogobangola was however giving me a tingling sensation in my spine; I was told that not far from here on the bank of the River Ganges Nawab Shirâjud Dawla was captured while he was escaping to Bihar; apparently, the boatman was instrumental in alerting his enemies. As an avid student of our Indian and Bengali history, I was very interested in that very sorry chapter. This is the general area where the Final Act of the drama in the history of independent Bengal was staged, its director: The Force of Destiny! Giuseppe Verdi could have composed his *La Forza del Destino* (the force of destiny) based on the meandering plots right here too. The main actor in this tragedy is the sovereign ruler of the states of Bengal, Bihar and Orissa - Nawab Mîrzâ Mohammad Shirâjud Dawla whom the Englishmen called him by his Anglici-zed name 'Sir Roger Dowlett' as they were not able to pronounce his correct name! In here took place the infamously decisive Battle of Polashi (Anglicized to Plassey) on 23 June 1757 on the bank of River *Bhagirothi* that eventually led to us being enslaved by the British for the next 190 some years.

Confession of a Terrorist!
Chapter 6   Target 6

The names Meer Modon, Mohon Lal, Meer Zafar, Ghasheti Begum, Yar Latif, and Rai Durlov etc. were going through my mind. While most have vilified Meer Zafar and lionized the Nawab, he on the other hand was no saint; far from it; he was impetuous, petulant, and quickly made a lot of enemies including and especially his close elder relatives. As uxorious as he was, he allegedly had the daughter-in-law of Manik Chand Jagath Seth – one of the two Marwari trader-banker brothers, ab-ducted; and attempted abduction of the daughter of Moharani of Natore. Is it surprising that there was no shortage of people to go after him, be disloyal to him? Why won't they take things personally? Did they think or know that their treachery would result in our cataclysmal slavery under the British for generations to come? Could Meer Zafar himself anticipate that he in turn would be betrayed by the British? The ultra-nationalists would be quick to lay the blame only on the foreigners or use the foreign ancestry as a convenient and self-deceiving scapegoat.

The Nawab was betrayed not just by Meer Zafar but many others, his close relatives included; both Indians and foreigners, or foreign-born or of foreign ancestry; negotiating the treachery was an Armenian merchant Khojah Petrus Nicholas. Then

Confession of a Terrorist!
Chapter 6   **Target 6**

there were the Marwari trader-banker brothers Mahtab Chand and Manik Chand Jagath Seth, who had only financial interest in their mind, although the abduction of a Jagath Seth girl did not help either. For bigotry, if one wants to blame their non-Bengali or foreign ancestry then why is the Nawab exempted? Nawab Shirâjud Dawla himself was Turkish-Arab [save our indigenous rulers who were overpowered hundreds of years ago, the rest of Indian rulers since then had been foreigners]. But that should not matter; they were Indians, most of them that is except the Armenian and the British. Can one blame only the foreigners, in this case the British and absolve the Indians of their treason? How about the French and the Dutch who later came to help Meer Zafar against the British in vain? Did the French and Dutch have the best interest of India in their mind, did the Indians, did anyone? One of the thickest plotted opera indeed; each Act taking an entire evening!

I could not stop ruminating. Both the admirers and critics point to the fact that the Nawab was enthroned at the age of 23; so what? Alexander the Great was even younger! That is no excuse; the patriotic Freedom Fighters that I had patched-up in Sector 2 were mostly in their teens and they showed more character than the Nawab. Did the fact that

Confession of a Terrorist!
Chapter 6   Target 6

his treasury was worth over £3,000,000 in those days made a young sovereign reckless? Didn't he have any responsibility for it, if not its lion share?

So why blame it all on Meer Zafar and to a lesser extent the British? We Indians let them have it; they coveted it and we handed it to them for a price. We must accept some responsibility.

Retrospectively we may choose to fault one or the other depending on our knowledge of history or lack thereof, and our prejudice. But the end result is nevertheless pathetic – 190 years of colonial exploitation; shifting the blame or finding a scapegoat does not alleviate the pain by an iota. I would however be remiss if I did not mention the few good that resulted from that though, e.g. my being able to compose this in English!

Notwithstanding the palace intrigues, and the weaknesses of the Nawab and the politics of the time, this was the beginning; yes, the dawning of the British rule in India; and sadly the end of ours as independent India. The British Empire under the guise of the so-called British East India Company looted the Bengal Treasury of over £3,000,000; Robert Clive personally took £234,000! Besides, the British now had access to the massive source of food-grains and taxes, allowing the British East India "Company" to significantly strengthen its military might. £3,000,000 may not sound much now, but consider its buying-power back then. As most if not all Indians know, this enormous bounty helped to kick-off the British colonial rule with concomitant mass economic exploitation and cultural domination in not just in India, but nearly all of South Asia. Following this critical battle in Polashi and those that followed strengthened the British foothold in South Asia and paved the way for British colonial rule in the rest of Asia. Alas, we are still paying the price; in India "more than 66% of the population in some regions experienced famine during British colonialism a century ago."[2]

I took the opportunity to visit Polashi (from the bright red flower *Polash*) and *Hazar Duari* the

---

[2] In the January-February 2010 issue of the *American Journal of Human Biology* volume 22 (1) pages 1-17 (published online in October 2009) Dr Jonathan CK Wells of the University College London report that the average height of Indian males dropped at a rate of 2 centimeters per century in the decades following British colonialism.
http://www.ncbi.nlm.nih.gov/pubmed/19844897?itool=EntrezSystem2.PEntrez.Pubmed.Pubmed_ResultsPanel.Pubmed_RVDocSum&ordinalpos=3 Please also see the article by Ann Gibbons in *Science* 11 December 2009 (volume 326 pages 1478-9) issue http://www.sciencemag.org/cgi/content/full/326/5959/1478)

Confession of a Terrorist!
Chapter 6   Target 6

palace of a thousand doors although only about 900 of them are real, in Murshidabad. In Baharampur I saw the *Nemok Haram Deori* (The Traitor's Gate) the spot where Nawab Shirâjud Dawla was killed; it is also near the place where William Watts met Meer Zafar to plot the treachery. A few months short of exactly a hundred years later, here in Baharampur the first major battle of the Sepoy Mutiny of 1857 was fought on the 25th of February 1857. And seven years hence during my visit to London I went to the Tower of London. There amongst many other treasures that the British colonials have "collected" or rather pillaged from various colonies was armor from the elephant of the Battle of Polashi! It was a very emotional moment for me; I could hardly control my tears let alone other feelings, such as my blood boiling.

On one of these most emotional trips we had to dash to board the train as it was just about to leave the station; we did not have the time to purchase the tickets and thought that we will do it in the train. The ticket checker walked into our car and as I was trying to give him the money to buy the tickets he recognized that we were from Bangladesh "you must be a *shoronarthi* (refugee)" and told me that we did not need to pay! Another example of the generosity and kindness of the

Confession of a Terrorist!
Chapter 6   Target 6

Government of India; the checker however seemed a bit irritated; perhaps this area being close to Kolkata there are a lot of us refugees and he just had enough; I was deeply embarrassed.

Qamrul Hassan (Raton)

Against the wishes and insistence of my hosts – Daliah's uncle and aunt, after 4-5 days I left for Kolkata, Daliah accompanied me but her politician brother Shelley stayed behind in the comfort and safety of his *Mama Bari*. In Kolkata there lived a friend of Daliah's aunt. We arrived at her apartment in Park Circus area at around 22:30 Hr. but no one was home. Not having any place to go and no one else we knew, we decided to wait; a little past midnight she came. Another difference; we could not imagine a single woman walking in the streets of Dhaka at midnight.

The next day we came to the Bangladesh Mission (former High Commission of Pakistan) that housed the government in exile. Here we met many friends and acquaintances, most notably my childhood buddy Raton, my cousin Shoaib and Maj. Nurul Islam. Qamrul Hassan, nicknamed Raton was my neighbor. He too had many siblings and I was friends to several of them. His parents were

Confession of a Terrorist!
Chapter 6   Target 6

some of the most wonderful people I knew; very loving and kind; Raton's mother – *Khalamma* liked me very much and I would never be able to leave their house without having a glass of nice hot milk (yes, she knew how much I like hot milk!) and some cookies; and of course, a glass of water afterwards to rinse my mouth! I would be playing with Raton and his brothers Khokon and Milon badminton or cricket every afternoon. Raton was also great for my ego. During my childhood, I had been very skinny, which did not bother me or my parents as much as it did their friends; my dad's friends would always ask Dad as to why he being a physician did not do anything to make me 'healthier.' But unhealthy I was not. As scrawny as I was, Raton was skinnier and again not unhealthy at all, just slim; I had someone to compare to and not feel bad. We had a very emotional greeting here in exile; I knew Raton had joined *Mukti Bahini* and I had not had a chance to say good bye to him when he left as you don't want anyone, even your best friends to know lest the Pakistan army finds out through torture; and torture they did.

This time it was a hello and goodbye at the same time, he was leaving that very moment for Dhaka to conduct some guerilla (or 'terrorist') operations.

Confession of a Terrorist!
Chapter 6　　　　　　　Target 6

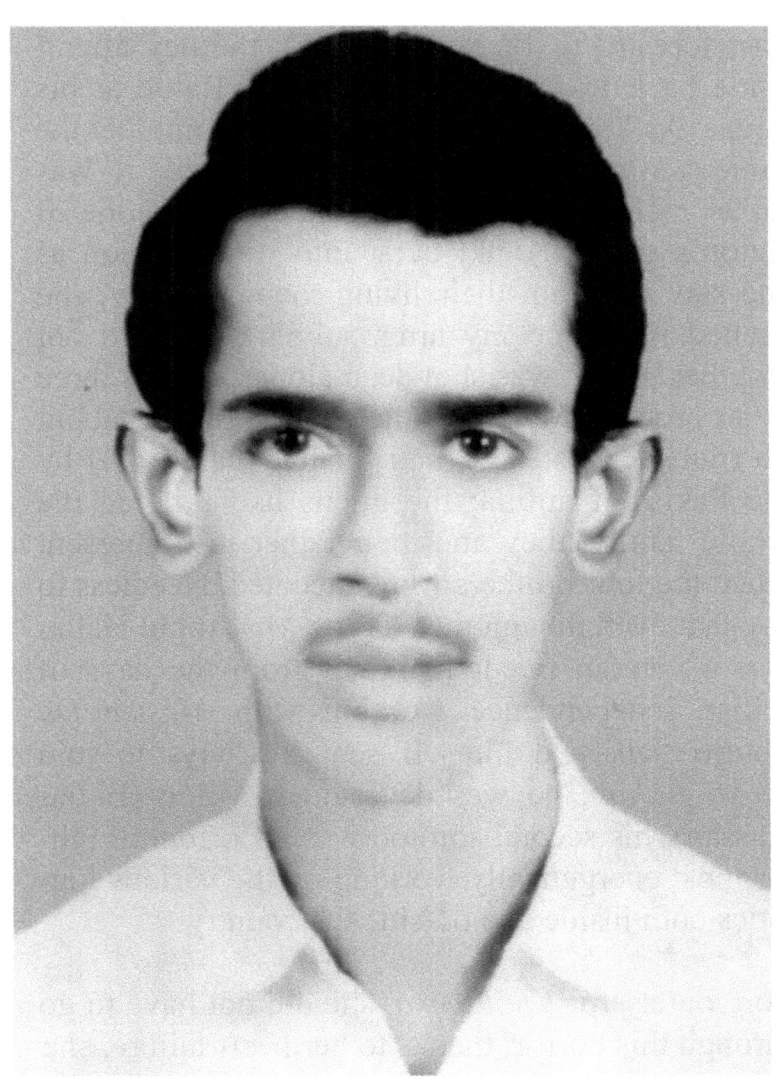

Raton (Qamrul Hassan)

Confession of a Terrorist!
Chapter 6   **Target 6**

Fast forward to 17 January 1972, the day after I came back to Dhaka, I went to see Raton at his house. As I approached his house I did not feel the same warmth and joyfulness as before, it was rather melancholic. I did not have to ask, one of Raton's sisters Khuki burst into wail as soon as she saw me from their living-room window, she dashed right into my arms sobbing; I could not stop her. Raton was shot dead along with his three other brothers Makhon - the eldest, 'Lucky' about 16 (not lucky at all!), and Shahar (barely 14) by the Pakistani militia; the goons had ordered the whole family, they and their father to be present when the four brothers were executed. Needless to say that even though their father Mr. Abdul Halim was a veteran freedom fighter from the days of Indian independence working with *Master Da* Shurjo Sen, and himself sent his boys to join *Mukti Bahini*, he was devastated. Milon (Ektiar Hassan), his second son too was a Freedom Fighter most energetically working on the various logistics both inside and outside the country.

Fortunately for *Khalamma,* she did not have to go through this horror; thanks to her heart failure, she

Confession of a Terrorist!
Chapter 6   Target 6

Iqbal Hassan (Shahar 14)   Rokibul Hassan (Lucky 16)

Bakhtiar Hassan (Makhon)   Ataur Rahman (Nehal)

had passed away a couple of years prior. That is another sad story by itself.

Confession of a Terrorist!
Chapter 6   Target 6

I was just beginning my clinical year in the Medical College. Of course, that does not matter to your family and friends; just because you're in medical college is good enough for them, to them you *are* a doctor! When *Khalamma* was having difficulty breathing, a local real medical doctor saw her and made the common misdiagnosis of it as asthma. Luckily, that was one of the first things our professor of Medicine Dr. Fazle Rabbee[3] had taught us. Owing to *Khalamma's* confidence in me, she refused the treatment for 'asthma' without having the opportunity of my (!) opinion. It was around 20:00 Hr. when Raton snatched me from my home, we ran to his house; I realized that her breathing difficulty was *cardiac* asthma because her heart was failing to pump blood resulting in water-logging in her lungs, literally drowning her. Epinephrine, the treatment for asthma would have killed her instantly.

We rushed her to the ER; she was correctly diag-

---

[3] Professor Fazle Rabbee was one of the most brilliant physicians who was brutally slain by the Pakistanis on 15 December 1971, a day before the final victory; his faults – he was a Bengali, a brilliant professor and an intellectual. Many other professors of various universities, especially the University of Dhaka and other intellectuals were systematically slaughtered by the Pakistani military and their *Razakar, Al Bodor and Al Shams* militias.

Confession of a Terrorist!
Chapter 6   Target 6

nosed by the ER physician and the appropriate medicines were given. What she needed urgently

Prof. Fazle Rabbee, Professor of Medicine, Dhaka Medical College, University of Dhaka (Source: Google)

Confession of a Terrorist!
Chapter 6 — Target 6

was a "rotating tourniquet"[4] which the ER did not have back then. Thus, she left us despite getting the correct diagnosis by her favorite 'doctor' medical student. It's a pity; during my internship in the USA starting from July of 1972 I had brought back innumerable patients from near death by this simple machine. As to Raton, my only consolation is that I did get a chance to say goodbye to one of my dearest friends, this time.

In May 2010, I went to visit his house in Teztori bazaar; I could barely recognize the neighborhood because of the overgrowth of housing not unlike elsewhere in Bangladesh. I had an idea of the general location of Raton's house; suddenly I saw a dilapidated yellowish signboard about 80 x 90 cm with the name of martyrs of the Liberation war:

> Bakhtiar Hassan (Makhon)
> Qamrul Hassan (Raton)
> Rokibul Hassan (Lucky)
> Iqbal Hassan (Shahar)
> Ataur Rahman (Nehal)

---

[4] This is an electrically operated machine that cuts-off the blood flow from one limb at a time to decrease the burden on the heart reducing the water-logging of the lungs.

Confession of a Terrorist!
Chapter 6   **Target 6**

The names of all the four brothers were listed in descending order according to their age. My beloved friend Raton was second; I put my fingers on his name, glided it a few times and before I was losing control of my emotion moved them away. In addition to the four brothers, there was also Ataur Rahman nicknamed Nehal; he was another neighborhood kid slaughtered by the Pakistanis on 14th December just 2 days before the victory day.

A Little Fuss
Honeymoon in Bus

At the Bangladesh Mission I could sense that a large scale operation and perhaps a full blown war between India and Pakistan were in the offing. During my very brief encounter with Maj. Nurul Islam in Sector 2, I was very impressed by him though I was not sure what it was. It may have been his demeanor, intelligence, his serious no-nonsense attitude combined with dry humor; he simply had this aura about him that made me have deep regard for him. I also don't know why but it seems that he liked me too. I wasn't sure what exactly Maj. Nurul Islam's portfolio was, but I suspected that he knew a lot about everything that had to do with our struggle and that he was one of the top people in the military think-tank. I asked

Confession of a Terrorist!
Chapter 6   Target 6

him about how to go to Sector 6; he was happy that I was going there. Then he asked me "are you going there by yourself or is Daliah going with you?" I did not know of Daliah's intentions; actually I had not asked her about it. Having gone through the drama in Sector 2, I wanted to breakup with her; to let her accompany me to Sector 6 was out of the question. Besides, she had her uncles also here in Kolkata with whom she could stay comfortably and I was no longer honor-bound to be her protector. Then came the most insightful of the advices "Shamsuddin, no one will recall what you have done or how much you have sacrificed for your country. If you and Daliah go to Sector 6 unmarried, the only thing people and history will remember about you is that you two unmarried youths slept together under the pretext of Liberation War. My advice is if she wants to go with you then you must get married."

I thought that that was very sage, coming from Maj. Nurul Islam, it was no surprise; but getting married now and especially after the recent events?! That was not even in the back of my mind. And since she now is in a safe and secure environment with and near her extended family, I felt that my pledge of being personally responsible for her life and safety is irrelevant. I asked

Confession of a Terrorist!
Chapter 6   Target 6

Daliah what her intentions were and she insisted that she wanted to go to Sector 6. Is it for adventure or is it out of devotion to her country? She said she too wanted to serve the country. That was an extraordinary display of patriotism on her part; at the tip of hat she was ready to sacrifice the safety and comfort of being in Kolkata for the unknown and risky life in the warfront. Do I have the right to deny her duty to her country? More importantly, do I have the right to deny my motherland of her services in time of its need? Time is of essence now as I could feel that large-scale military operations are imminent; I may have gotten some of the feeling from Raton's hurried departure as well. Reluctantly I told her that in this case we need to get married and told her Maj. Nurul Islam's farsighted advice; she too saw through the wisdom. She asked one of her uncles - her father's cousin Mr. Sikandar Abu Zafar, a poet. As per the Bengali culture where elders command respect and authority over the younger siblings, Mr. Abu Zafar being elder to her father did not feel uncomfortable in getting us married in lieu of her father who was back in Saatkhira in the occupied Bangladesh. The wedding was set for the next day 12 November.

Confession of a Terrorist!
Chapter 6   Target 6

Enter my cousin Shoaib. His mother was my dad's younger sister. Shoaib's family used to live in the village in Noakhali about 2 km or so from my grandparents' and I would be visiting them every time I would go to visit my grandparents. Shoaib was about a year or less older than I; we were great friends, we both got along very well with each other more than we did with our own siblings! I guess that's what cousin relationships are – close but not too close for comfort. Like my friend Raton, he too had several siblings with whom I was very close too. But, A. H. M. Shoaib[5]

---

[5] Like my name, Shoaib's and his brothers had three initials for First and Middle names. Unlike many other cultures Bengalis have used a wide variety of names, often borrowed from different languages depending on their attractiveness, trend of the time and after famous people. So it is not surprising that some children were named Churchill, Hitler, Lenin, Gagarin, Gogol etc. During the period my cousins and I were born, the Indian independence movement was at its zenith. Perhaps our parents like few others wanted to honor the Moslem leaders such as Abul Kalam Azad, hence A. K. It became the trend to have 3 first initials: A.H. M., A. B. M., etc. M representing Mohammed to make sure that our identities as Moslems are unmistakable; the Moslems in India were fighting their own battle for a separate country called Pakistan so their identity as Moslems was very important to them. As to the Family name, that too has not been frequently propagated amongst Moslem progeny of East Bengal. Shamsuddin is a hybrid name created by my father by combining the first name of my mother <u>Shamsun</u> to his last name Abe<u>din</u> as a token of their love; perhaps he also wanted to make sure that my name bears the

Confession of a Terrorist!
Chapter 6   **Target 6**

was one of my most favorite cousins. Then one day he left for West Pakistan to go to Pakistan Air Force Public School in Lower Topa and on to Risalpur Pakistan Air Force Academy. We grew apart as he was far away; our schedules did not cooperate when he came on vacations as the demand of college and medical college on me was extremely high. He became a Pakistan Air Force officer. Being concerned about his safety and wellbeing after 25th March, while he was in a radar station in West Pakistan, his elder brother had sent him a fabricated telegram stating that his father was mortally ill or something like that. With that, he was given a leave of absence to go to Noakhali; from there he crossed the border near Feni and finally on to the Bangladesh Mission in Kolkata. In here, he was my only relative and friend. Thus, I invited him to be a guest at my wedding the next day. "But I have no money to give you a gift" was his response! I gave him about 30 some Rupees and told him to show up with a gift; our family pride is at stake here!

This was my first trip ever to Kolkata and I heard a lot about it; there are so many places to go, so

---

identity of both of my parents! Unlike most cultures, friends are not always addressed by their first name, especially amongst the Bengali Moslems.

much to do, but I was not in any mood for sightseeing, nor was there any time for a war was going on and I am almost <u>a</u>bsent <u>with</u>out <u>l</u>eave (AWOL). I however wanted to see the famous Howrah Bridge, especially because during the India-Pakistan war of 1965 the Pakistani propaganda machinery fed us with the news that the Pakistan Air Force had blown it off. Since I had to go shopping for my wedding to New Market, I made a detour and went to see the Bridge. Obviously 6 years after that war, I did not see any evidence of the bridge being blown off, perhaps it was repaired; but everyone I asked seemed bemused with my question, some even scoffed at me as the Howrah Bridge was never hurt!

The two gold guineas that I had were cashed, with which I bought a ring and some other bare necessities to meet the formalities at a minimum. Though I had attended several weddings in the past I was not privy to the 'behind the door' discussions; this was the first time I have been exposed so closely to what marriage really is. The discussions that I heard seemed more like a business negotiation and contract than a romantic "life together for as long as we live etc., etc." There was a stipulation that I must give my wife Daliah 100,001 [Indian] Rupees if we get a divorce and so on.

Confession of a Terrorist!
Chapter 6   **Target 6**

Any feeling of romanticism I had vanished by the time we were married, that is in the next minute – the time it took me to sign on the "dotted line." Twenty six years later I ended up in giving her several hundred times as much, only in monetary terms, let alone other direct and indirect considerations.

We spent that night in a small hotel; the next day we travelled about 70 km or so north to Bashirhat (opposite the border to Saatkhira in Bangladesh where Daliah's father's family came from) to visit another of her uncles. Her father's younger brother was a Member of the Parliament from Saatkhira. Her cousin (father's sister's son) Mr. Shafi Ahmed Islam was also in politics. An aspiring politician, Islam was looking after our refugees in the camp with earnest; observing his devotion and assiduousness for the welfare of our refugees was a breath of fresh air for it was at variance with most politicians; he appeared quite genuine. Herein again, the refugees were clearly from inside the neighboring districts of Bangladesh and not 'imported from the slums of Kolkata' as has been either ignorantly and/or maliciously claimed by some. They may have been from the slums of Kolkata; but the little that *I* saw, there was no evidence that these destitute were from any place

Confession of a Terrorist!
Chapter 6   Target 6

other than Bangladesh. Besides, Islam knew most, if not all of them. This was Sector 9 - commanded by Maj. Jalil. Apparently most of the military activities were guerilla warfare inside Khulna, Jessore and Borishal districts. I did not see any Freedom Fighters or *Mukti Bahini* camps here as in Sector 2. We stayed the night and on the following day on 14 November we got up very early to take another bus for a daylong trip to Shiliguri.

Sunset High in the Sky

The events of the last few days were emotionally and physically draining; thus I slept through most of the bus-trip till we arrived in Shiliguri. At the bus station in Shiliguri we took a taxi for Tetulia; unlike the train station, in here almost everyone knew how to go to Tetulia. The taxi driver was thrilled with the idea that he was coming inside Bangladesh. A kilometer or so past the city center bus station, from the outskirts of Shiliguri the road became narrow to a single-lane, and went through dense vegetation. The sun was setting, the hills and the tall trees on both sides of the road made it hard to enjoy the beauty of a setting sun. A lot of things were going through my mind. At least when I was going to Sonamura I had a guide who was not only a trained Freedom Fighter but also

Confession of a Terrorist!
Chapter 6   Target 6

very knowledgeable about the terrain, the danger spots, anticipated trouble etc. But here 'the lame leading the blind' I was the 'lame' leading my newlywed wife the 'blind.' Suddenly to my ecstasy I see a red setting sun, but it's high up in the sky! It was a red sun with golden map of Bangladesh on a bottle-green flag fluttering high on the tallest bamboo that I have seen; the flag was clearly a head and shoulder above the rest of the trees! We arrived at the Bangladesh Border Checkpoint. It was a small outpost about 2x2 m tin-shed housing with two sentries with walkie-talkies, a barrier across the road and of course the flag. I had seen the Bangladesh flag in Melaghor Head-Quarter of Sector 2, but that was in Indian Territory; this is Bangladesh and for real. It was just as thrilling to us as it was to the taxi-driver. I must confess that traveling in a dark road away from the city and into the jungles with my bride made me apprehensive about our safety; after all, there are stories of acts of violence involving taxi-drivers and their passengers: mugging, kidnapping, killing etc. But the sight of the Bangladesh flag and the checkpoint dissipated any of that instantly.

This is the first tangible evidence of Bangladesh with a real border checkpoint. When I had crossed the border in Saldanadi in Sector 2, I was greeted in a different manner, albeit no less breathtaking - the sweet air of my homeland that gushed on my face. But there was no proper entry to an independent country; there was no distinct demarcation where India ends and Bangladesh begins, no formality; we entered like we were trespassers or smugglers. We walked with caution not to provoke the Pakistani artillery gunners not too far, to shell on us. In contrast, here I was in a taxi, the outside air was cold and so the windows were up; I couldn't smell the sweet air of my motherland; but that has been compensated times and times over by that simple symbol: the checkpoint with the flag; we are not interlopers, we are entering our sovereign country as its citizens with dignity and self-respect, may even be pride.

But pride? That had been a feeling I have not felt for quite some time. Happy always; well, almost always; ecstatic - occasionally; but pride no, though some of my acquaintances may disagree. I had skipped Classes I and II, and entered the Rotary Primary School in Razabazar, Tezgaon, Dhaka, in Class III over the objection of the Headmaster. One of the teachers, an important one - Mr. Ilias, was a friend of my father and thus was familiar with me as he had observed Dad's home-teaching. His threat of resignation finally allowed me to be admitted even though I was younger than the required age. As usual, few weeks later we had our first examination and the test-papers were given back to us with scores after a few days. Half way between the school and our house there lived a hermit in a pit. While I was passing the recluse, something happened; I took out the exam papers and wanted to see my score. It was 49/50 in a non-math subject. Boy! Was I happy? Overjoyed, I danced the rest of the way – about a kilometer or so; dashed to my father who too was equally happy. With a voice of encouragement, he then told me that inasmuch as I did well, very well indeed, I could have done even better, it could have been a perfect score! That was the first, but certainly not the last time Dad had coached me on ego; his oft repeated words were "don't be a big fish in a little pond; try to swim in the ocean, see if you can even survive." Once when I recounted that incidence, someone [identity withheld] had deprecatingly told me that my father was being unkind and that sort of attitude could have hurt my ego. On the contrary, I could see Dad's point and always tried to do even better, a trait I have strived to develop subsequently. I saw the fruit of that doctrine during my PhD dissertation and writing subsequent scientific papers; no matter how many times I had carefully read and re-read,

Confession of a Terrorist!
Chapter 6   **Target 6**

my mentor and/or I would find ways to improve my thesis, humbling me each time. I am sure readers will find some errors in this very book even though I had gone through it many times. And I never ever seen or heard Dad showing pride or being boastful. So, pride is not something that I had felt often, but this time, YES Dad! Though I had nothing to do with this accomplishment – the creation of a new nation, I felt proud to be a Bengali. But, why should I be proud?

Did I fight for this piece of land and make it part of the liberated Bangladesh? Did I establish this checkpoint and/or raise the flag in the midst of a gun-battle with the enemy? It did not matter that we had that swath of land that only for strategic reasons the Pakistani military decided was not worth defending and fighting for so that we Bengalis could have it; but I felt proud nonetheless. May be Dad is right, that's why pride is illogical, but so is emotion. It is hard to control one's emotion, especially on matters such as this – logic has no place here Dad. Or, is it just ecstasy like my first exam grade and not pride since you taught me how not to be?

After my conversation with Maj. Nurul Islam in Kolkata, he had sent a message to Sq. Ldr. Sadru-

Confession of a Terrorist!
Chapter 6   **Target 6**

ddin the Sub-Sector commander, about our planned arrival; the sentries seemed to have been expecting us and directed the taxi driver as to where to take us. We drove through the road, now unpaved but hard surfaced somewhat like a gravel (as opposed to stone-chips these were brick-chunks or *khoa* in Bānglā) road for another 2-3 km of exhilarating journey; a mixture of emotions: adventure of entering into a place I have never been to, pride - to be entering my motherland with dignity, conviction that I won't be terrorized in this part of my motherland, excitement for the opportunity that lies ahead for me to aid my fellow countrymen, and all the other positive feelings filled my mind. We arrived at a majestic old white colonial building on the northern outskirt of Tetulia. This was a Rest House for the Government officers. We were warmly greeted by Mrs. Shirin Bashar, the wife of Sector Commander, an Air Force officer - Wing Commander Khademul Bashar, and their two daughters Shompa and Ika.

Wing Commander Bashar

We had a sumptuous dinner. Around 22:00 Hr. Wing Cmdr. Bashar showed up from his HQ; he was expecting our arrival, so he came to greet us

Confession of a Terrorist!
Chapter 6 — Target 6

personally! With short hair, a bit curly and, well-trimmed moustache that was very proportionate to his handsome face, he had a very imposing figure; tall, straight as an arrow with sharp facial features and eyes that emanate brilliance, strength, valor, determination, and humor. He was extremely pleasant and gracious; we had a good conversation. But there was no pretension in his statements, all matters of fact. He enjoyed Scotch very much and was drinking that, straight. He dispelled any notion I ever had about the social stigma of excessive drinking; he was drinking the Scotch at an even pace over the next couple of hours; my keen medical observation did not detect any sign of mood or behavioral change no matter how subtle they might have been. This is another lesson that I learnt in the 'field' that one doesn't get to learn in medical college: tolerance to alcohol can be quite varied and there are 'supermen' amongst us who can enjoy it without getting tipsy.

About 7-8 months later in the United States of America where I was doing my Internship training at Lawrence General Hospital, an acquaintance of mine philosophized that most people drink alcohol to get drunk; under the pretext of that they do things they always wanted to do, but could not have done without alcohol as their deeds would

Confession of a Terrorist!
Chapter 6   Target 6

Wing Cmdr. Khademul Bashar, Sector Commander - Sector 6, later Air Vice-Marshal and Chief of Bangladesh Airforce.
(Source: Google)

not have been socially acceptable. They know very well what they did, but give the excuse that they were under the influence of alcohol; they were drunk; it's a state of mind. How profound!

Confession of a Terrorist!
Chapter 6   Target 6

This was a college kid who was working at the hospital as a janitor during the summer holidays to support himself. Of course, the pharmacological effects of alcohol are unquestionable; but the psychological effects can perhaps be modulated by the strength of one's mind and presence or lack of hid-den agenda. Clearly, Wing Cmdr. Bashar had no hidden agenda; he was forthright, had a very strong mind and straight-talking; pharmacologically speaking, most likely his alcohol-metabolizing enzymes were induced to great efficiency (a common response by the body); alcoholic he was *not*. So, not long after the independence when he died in a plane crash which he was flying allegedly under the influence of alcohol (a very convenient and plausible pretext for the gullible), I for one cannot accept that nonsense of an excuse; for I have seen him time and time again, and up close. But who staged this "accident" and why? This is another of the tragic deaths that the nation has 'swept under the rug.'

Shortly after midnight we went to bed. By the time I woke up and headed for breakfast, Wing Cmdr. Bashar was gone! Mrs. Bashar told me that he left for the Head-Quarter at 05:00! Is this a man who had about 200 mL of Scotch only 5 hours prior?! Graciously he came to welcome us, but duty's call did not allow him to spend any time with his beloved wife and two most adorable daughters. Such is duty, honor and sacrifice for one's country – patriotism.

In the morning light in the distance I could see the snow-capped Himalaya on the north from the Rest House which was on a higher ground than the farm-land to the west. From this vantage point the river Mahananda with its riverbed a bit dried-up, less than a kilometer to the west and north, was adding to the beauty of the landscape. My enjoyment of the splendor was almost immediately interrupted – Sq. Ldr. Sadruddin came soon after and took me for orientation; no nonsense, no time to spare, get on with the business, but pleasant.

CHAPTER 7

DREAM COME TRUE

As all good military leaders and strategists, Squadron Leader Sadruddin Hossain was no less cognizant of the importance of good medical support for his troops. Like that in Sector 2, the *Mukti Bahini* fighters were again composed of the 'regular' trained personnel – remnant of the East Pakistan Rifles (EPR) and defected Pakistani military, and the young men mostly in their teens who volunteered to fight for the independence of their motherland. In contrast to Sector 2 however, I had not seen any cases of malaria perhaps because there were very few mosquitoes. That may be due to the fact that the dense jungles of Tripura were a fertile breeding heaven for the mosquitoes. Though I had

Confession of a Terrorist!
Chapter 7 Dream Come True

seen occasional cases of diarrhea, it was not certainly as common in here as it was in Sector 2.

An abandoned school house about 3-4 km southwest from Tetulia in the Kachabari area was a makeshift hospital. There were about 8-10 patients who had a wide spectrum of illnesses, but only one or two with combat injury. Dr. Atiur Rahman, a senior, middle-aged physician was tending to the patients once a day or every other day[1]. He had his own practice and was not dedicated to the hospital fulltime; neither the patient volume nor the lack of compensation justified that, I suppose. He was however doing his patriotic duty to aid our boys. In charge of the hospital, patient dining, medical and other supplies was a Havildar[2] from the EPR, who

---

[1] Aside from the MBBS degree there was an accelerated and abbreviated program for producing health care professionals in East Pakistan administered at the Mitford Hospital in Dhaka. The graduates had a LMF (Licentiate of Medical Faculty) degree which restricted their professional advancement; they could however subsequently enroll in a specific program to receive their full licensure as an MBBS physician by taking a "Condensed" course. If my memory serves right, Dr. Atiur Rahman had gone through such a program, but I am not certain about this as I had very little interaction with him.

[2] Havildar is a non-commissioned officer above the rank of a common soldier – approximately equivalent to Corporal in US Army.

had some medical training. The "Medical Supply Room" was almost bare; there were no medicine, not even the commonly used painkillers, antibiotics, let alone surgical instruments. A few packages of surgical gauze and some antiseptic lotion was all there was. The intensity of combat operation here appeared to be less than that in Sector 2, at least judging by the number of combat wounded Freedom Fighters.

Mr. Sirkar of Indian Red Cross, Shiliguri

While at the Bangladesh Mission in Kolkata, I had sensed that a largescale military action was about to happen. In here I was getting that even more, though Sq. Ldr. Sadruddin as a good commander did not or would not divulge any information. However, he could not hide the tone of urgency during his conversations with me. It was evident that he wanted the medical care to be efficient and immediately. That made me even more suspicious that the situation was about to change, rapidly; it was 'also in the air' like 'calm before the storm.' Sq. Ldr. Sadruddin's voice also reflected his frustration with the status of medical care. He had told me that each week he gave several thousand Indian

Confession of a Terrorist!
Chapter 7   Dream Come True

Rupees to the Havildar for medicine and supplies; yet the following week there would be none left. "How much money do you want to buy what you require to make the operation run efficiently?" very generously and genuinely he asked. I declined to put a monetary figure; instead I wanted him to take me to Shiliguri where we could purchase some necessary surgical instruments like scissors, forceps, suturing needles, sutures, etc., which he did. At the surgical supplies store I had asked the shopkeeper to show us the way to the local Red Cross Office.

Mr. Sirkar was the director of the Indian Red Cross in Shiliguri. His office was responsible for the welfare of the hundreds of thousands of refugees who were crammed up in so many Refugee Camps all over his district. Red Cross's mandate was clear; it is there for the refugees and not to aid political organization. Sounds familiar?! But, I did not have to make the same argument to Mr. Sirkar as I did to the Christian Missionaries in Sector 2 in Sonamura. Mr. Sirkar was not just kind and gentle showing extremely gracious hospitality, he was just as thrilled to have met us. He too like the rest of the people in India had heard about *Mukti Bahini,* but he never saw one. He was in for a treat; for the first time, he got to see not one, but two including a commander, an Air Force Officer, and his doctor!

Confession of a Terrorist!
Chapter 7   Dream Come True

He was willing to give his whole store away, literally! Most enthusiastically he invited us to his home and to meet his family, an offer we had to graciously decline due to the lateness of the hour. Somewhat saddened, he instructed his manager to "give these two gentlemen all they need." The manager who was very much aware of the rules reminded his boss as to the fact that the *Mukti Bahini* is from Bangladesh and he has no official capacity to send aid there. While that caused an acute consternation in both Sq. Ldr. Sadruddin and me, it was however very short lived; to our disbelief and ecstasy he replied "why don't you write down Tetulia Refugee camp?"

After we had finished tea and snacks with Mr. Sirkar we walked to the store room with the Manager. Unlike the store room in GB Hospital in Agartala where Capt. Akhtar and I were set up to steal the medical supplies, here we were given a legitimate free hand. We took all the necessary supplies we needed and more! It was mid-November; being up north, close to the Himalayas it started to get chill. A stockpile of colorful blankets caught my eyes. Growing up in a tropical country admittedly I have not seen too many varieties of blankets; we hardly needed them. These blankets were made of high quality wool, were very warm and came in

Chapter 7   Dream Come True

different patterns and bright colors. Sensing that I was attracted to the pile of blankets the Manager asked us if we needed any! Hmm! What an interesting idea! The total patient-bed capacity we had was about 20; so we asked for 20. Very kindly he gave us 22 - the two additional ones, one each for Sq. Ldr. Sadruddin and me! Here is this bureaucrat who only a few minutes ago was concerned about strictly adhering to the rules and regulation; now in contrast he effuses his love for the needy, fellow Bengalis, fellow human beings! It was very touching. Sq. Ldr. Sadruddin and I were traveling in an American-made Jeep CJ5 or CJ6 I can't recall. It was a vehicle for the Pakistan Military officers that the rebels brought with them; it was not meant to be a pickup van or truck to carry supplies. Our Jeep was overflowing with what we got in one day (and with an open and ardent invitation to come whenever we need to); we had to drive carefully not to lose any of our bounty.

The patients were very excited to see and actually use those blankets. It not only helped them combat the chills of November but had boosted their morale so much so that 90% of their ailments had evaporated instantly. It was very gratifying to see their joy.

Confession of a Terrorist!
Chapter 7   Dream Come True

The Enemy Within

A couple of days later, Sq. Ldr. Sadruddin asked me whether I would like to visit his den in Bhajanpur. There, at the outskirt of the village near the Tetulia-Panchagarh road he had set up his Head-Quarter. It was a small tin-shed house with two beds and a desk with a set of wireless communication equipment. His personnel were in another house where there were more of the communication equipment, arms and ammunitions – rather typical of the few Sub-Sector HQs that I have had the privilege of seeing. The supper was delicious. It seemed that he had remembered what he had promised me back in Sector 2 in order to entice me here. Everything was as fresh as they could be. In my honor he had asked the cook to prepare chicken[3] and other special dishes; a live chicken was procured from the local farmer, sacrificed and cooked, all within an hour. That's as fresh as it can be! Even the rice was prepared in a special manner (*polao*) as in celebratory dinners.

The next day he decided to accompany me during my round to the hospital. Having had experience

---

[3] For readers besides Bengalis, chicken and carp are delicacies served to honored guests

Confession of a Terrorist!
Chapter 7   Dream Come True

with 'disappearance' of our hard-earned supplies in Sector 2, I took Sq. Ldr. Sadruddin*'s* concern about the constant complains of supply-shortage by the Havildar, seriously; we walked to the Store Room. Not to my surprise, but certainly to Sq. Ldr. Sadruddin's, most of the medicine we procured had banished! Incense may be an understatement to describe his reaction. The Havildar had followed us tiptoed, perhaps he wanted to see if his mischief would go undetected and was behind us. Sq. Ldr. Sadruddin turned to him and asked for an explanation; there was none except a vacant stare. Boom... Boom, the bolts from the blue, several Air Force punches landed on the Havildar's not-so-innocent face. Suffice it to say that the supplies stopped disappearing hence!

For the Pakistan military, this peninsular area of free Bangladesh territory north of Panchagarh may not have been strategically worth fighting for. This swath of flat farmland of bright yellow mustard crop was dotted with green villages. As you can see from the map, the area south of Panchagarh is much wider and now not only easier but also worth defending by the Pakistanis. Thus the northern-most position of the Pakistan army was at Panchagarh.

Confession of a Terrorist!
Chapter 7   Dream Come True

Beginning the 3rd week of November '71, the *Mukti Bahini* started to turn up the heat on the Pakistani army by shelling them. The Indian army was not anywhere near; they wanted Bangladesh Liberation army, the *Mukti Bahini* to have some fun. In preparation we had dug a 4 x 5 m hole in the ground in the middle of tall bamboo bushes of a village within about 2 km from the Pakistan army position. This was covered by a tent; Daliah and I set up the emergency treatment facility there. In its usual barbaric manner, the mighty Pakistan army not only fought our *Mukti Bahini*, but also started to 'gallantly' shell the village where our frontline medical facility was! One would expect the villagers to be terrified and turned against us; no! They failed to terrorize these docile otherwise peace-loving peasants!

The unfazed village women were watching Daliah assisting me while I was removing the shrapnel and bullets from our Freedom Fighters with amazement and even amusement; amused because they had not seen, nor expected to see a city girl wearing trousers, in a remote village at the war-front up-close to the enemy-line and serving the Freedom Fighters. They asked my wife whether I was her "*Vaathar*" a term I heard for the first time. In local colloquial terms it means husband – someone who provides

Confession of a Terrorist!
Chapter 7   Dream Come True

Vaath or rice - the provider. They giggled a bit, but felt inspired to help, an offer I had graciously considered. But there was no time for us to train them; casualties were coming in as fast as they could. Assisted by Daliah, I patched most of them up; there were a couple of patients with serious injuries requiring amputation of legs which were beyond my abilities, they were sent to Baghdogra Indian Military Base Hospital. The thunderous roar of the Pakistani artillery returning the fire in response to our mortars was deafening, not to mention of the occasional Cluster Bombs that exploded midair overhead. However, the dense bamboo trees provided us and the villagers some protection. The village-girls had to be satisfied with giving us other supporting help the best way they could such as bringing drinking water to the wounded, offering them snacks and words of comfort, bring boiling water for sterilizing the surgical instruments etc.

More Volunteers

Hurrah! After a day-long fight the valiant Pakistani Army was in retreat! *Mukti Bahini* had inflicted heavy casualties on them. They found that it was too costly for them to stay where they were; their military strategy including trying to terrorize

Chapter 7   Dream Come True

the innocent villagers did not work. Under Sq. Ldr. Sadruddin's command our forces made frontal attacks and had pushed them about 2 km to the rear in south towards Thakurgaon, but still in Panchagarh area; they were north of Panchagarh, now they retreated to the south of it. So I closed my hole in the ground of a frontline treatment facility and also moved forward to the south along with the advancing *Mukti Bahini*. That I was moving forward along with (but right behind) our troops made me feel like we were chasing the powerful Pakistani army run away. For the first time, I was experiencing what it was like wining a battle even though I had not done any fighting.

The village-girls were not the only ones that wanted to volunteer. There were others. By this time, four or five young men, ranging from 18 to 21 years of age, all BA or BSc students of Rajshahi University, except the oldest who was a Master's student came to me to volunteer. Given the rapid surge in combat injury, I certainly could use additional help. I trained them in basic emergency management and they just as quickly mastered the techniques; they became quite good at it. We had set up our hospital about 2 km north of the Pakistan Army position in an abandoned house, can't recall exactly what it was, but most likely a Primary

Confession of a Terrorist!
Chapter 7   Dream Come True

School on the Bhajanpur-Panchagarh road. The sounds of our mortars and the enemy's artillery fire nearby were the telltale evidence that the fight was going on. But we felt quite secure and very confident that the enemy will not be returning here, ever. We also felt a sense of great accomplishment and conquest since this area we had just moved in was liberated from the Pakistani military through battle; our forces beat the enemy and became victorious. Ecstasy was perhaps an understatement to describe my happiness, for the contentment was redoubled owing to the pent-up frustration of not being able to be in my motherland; and now we were triumphant; we forced the enemy to retreat and conquered our land, no matter how small that area may have been. I, for the first time was experiencing what all other victorious armies felt. It was blissful; that night Daliah and I made love for the first time!

In this area, the battle lasted two or three more days before the Pakistan army was on the run again. But before that they inflicted some additional casualties. One of them was a young man who used to be a first or second year student at Dhaka Medical College who was trained in an Indian Military Academy, then joined the Bangladesh Liberation Army as 2nd Lt Matin. He happened to be the younger brother of my friend from Notre Dame College, Dhaka,

Confession of a Terrorist!
Chapter 7   Dream Come True

Capt. Salek of Sector 2, Sub-Sector commander of Shaldanadi where the Pakistan Army riddled the body of a 14-year old Freedom Fighter. Fresh from his military training as a commissioned officer, Lt. Matin was impatient to kill the enemy; he was leading his soldiers in the battle up close, too close to the Pakistan Army position, got hit by shrapnel and came to me with a huge gaping laceration (cut) about 10 cm in length, 2-3 cm deep and wide open in the back of his upper thigh and buttock. Matin was slim, actually pretty skinny; so for him a 2-3 cm deep cut is quite deep indeed. The cut has gone through the thin layer of yellowish fatty tissue deep into the beefy red muscle underneath with blood gushing out. He was pleasantly surprised to have seen me; we knew each other in Dhaka Medical College despite the fact that he was several years junior to me, but he did not expect to see me here. He seemed reassured. Fortunately it was not in a vital part of the body. I had to stop the bleeding first and in a hurry, and then stitched him up; the suturing part was taking long as I had to carefully bring the lacerated ends of the muscles together, layer by layer and use a different absorbable suture material than the ones used for skin. Every minute or so he would be asking me "are you done yet?" "Not yet, Matin" I replied every time with a smile. Having experienced the zeal of other young Freedom Figh-

Confession of a Terrorist!
Chapter 7   Dream Come True

ters in Sector 2, I was not the least bit bothered. I knew he was impatient. No sooner I had sewed him up he stood up, picked up his Indian sub-machine gun and was ready to head for the front! "Oh NO, you are NOT going anywhere" putting my hand on his shoulder and resolutely pushing him down to sit, I said emphatically with a firm voice, unsmilingly this time. And I had given him strict order not to walk around as that could cause the stitches to give up and open-up the wound again. That would be a great setback as it would delay the healing process by weeks if not months. Visibly, he was not happy.

Matin was impetuous and becoming more so by every passing day; he just wanted to go back to the front and kill more Pakistani soldiers; he loathed to be sitting around or laying in bed in this shack of a hospital hearing the sounds of artillery fires in the distance; it seemed that the sound of gunfire was alluring him. How could I blame him for being restive to go back and fight? I empathized with his frustration; but without adequate immobilization, he could end up having complications; so, for the time being he will have to defer his yearning to kill a few more Pakistanis.

Anyway, the day after the Pakistan Army's 'heroic' retreat there was relative lull in the area and the

Confession of a Terrorist!
Chapter 7   Dream Come True

hospital. I had instructed my cadre of medical assistants to relax and be at ease after they had finished their duties and responsibilities especially since they were overworked during the past 48 hours of intense fighting; so, they did on this day. I had to go to Shiliguri to bring some more medical supplies and when I came back to the hospital late in the afternoon I immediately sensed a very tense situation in the air. The senior-most of my volunteers, the Master's student was outside the hospital sitting on the grass and crying silently. The mood of the others was poignant as well. It seems that though 2nd Lt Matin had received his military education in an Indian Military College, the damage the undemocratic Pakistani military government had inflicted on us remained permanently ensconced in our brains and 2nd Lt Matin was no exception. He had expected my civilian volunteer medical assistants to be on attention all the time and salute him at every opportunity etc. In my childhood days, I had accompanied my grandfather to some of his late-night mediation sessions. His practice of the deadly combination of absolute fairness, subtle diplomacy and firm resolve did not go unnoticed; I took a page from that book of his to tackle the situation. I lectured Matin that firstly the Freedom Fighters working as medical assistants reported to me and me only. Secondly, they were civilian volunteers

Confession of a Terrorist!
Chapter 7 Dream Come True

(as I reasoned with Lt. Col. Khaled Musharraf in Sector 2) and are not in the military the way he was and therefore he did neither have any authority on them, nor did they have any obligation to salute him. Thirdly, in this 'hospital' he was simply a patient and nothing more; the Freedom Fighters were there to help him as his equal. Finally, [the heavy artillery] each of the volunteer Freedom Fighters were just as educated if not more than he was; I pointed out to him that indeed the one whom he offended was a Master's student, way more educated than he was. Bengali society back then considered education to be the most important attribute in an individual, over financial, political or other factors. Thus, to his credit, Matin saw through this and apologized; that followed by my compliments on the great performance and hard works of the volunteers; along with some affectionate gestures they were appeased; 2nd Lt Matin was less happy, but got over it quickly.

Relentless Retreat

The next day we moved the hospital to the town of Panchagarh proper on the southern end in a Rural Health Center about 2 km from the Sugar Mill. This was the first Rural Health Center in East Pakistan

Confession of a Terrorist!
Chapter 7   Dream Come True

that I had seen and the physical plant looked rather good though quite small. It was a relatively new building with cream-colored exterior walls and neatly whitewashed interior, with a dispensary, storeroom, kitchen and a small patient ward that could house up to 10 patients or so. But there was no physician; the paramedical personnel told me that the physician-in-charge had left quite some time ago as the armed conflict in the area was intensifying. The clinic had virtually no medicine or medical supplies, only the building served as 'roof over our head;' but, it was a step above what we have been used to. Compared to the equivalent Health Center in Melaghor in Tripura (Sector 2), this is dismal in terms of the ability to provide care both as regards medicine and supplies, and professional coverage. I was disappointed that the only physician had left town presumably for his own safety. Who would take care of the needs of the people? That seemed quite selfish and contrary to the pledge we as physicians have made to humanity. On the other hand, finding the storeroom rather empty, I could not help but empathize with him; what could he do with his two bare hands? Hopefully it was the imminent sense of frustration and not selfish motive of his personal safety that drove him away.

Confession of a Terrorist!
Chapter 7 Dream Come True

The mighty Pakistan army was on the run again. After another two or three days, we moved to Saathkhamar along with our advancing Bangladesh Liberation Army. In Saathkhamar, we stayed in a High School building for two days. Since Takurgaon was a major town that was strategically important, the Pakistani military had put up stiff resistance. Not to be dissuaded, our fighters fought fiercely resulting in a lot of casualties; fortunately, none of them serious, they were mostly bullet and shrapnel wounds in non-vital parts of the body. Having those volunteer medical assistants was a great help. Not only they worked tirelessly, but they did it also with great alacrity and showed absolutely no sign of fatigue; I am indebted to them. In here, I had recovered [and saved] at least 30 of the bullets and shrapnel. 2nd Lt Matin has been ambulatory. Owing to the need of hospital beds for drastically increased number of casualties he was sent to his unit; not to miss the action to his glee he had rejoined them in chasing the defeated enemy. The Pakistani military was finally purged from Thakurgaon; following its liberation, we arrived there on the 30th November.

Around 27 or 28th November during the intense battle, to encourage and expedite the retreat of the Pakistan military, the Indian Air Force (IAF) star-

Chapter 7   Dream Come True

ted to provide air support to the *Mukti Bahini*. The oxymoronic 'friendly fire' seems to like Sq. Ldr. Sadruddin too much; his jeep was mistaken for a Pakistan military vehicle on retreat and strafed by the IAF! One can't help but wonder what is with Sq. Ldr. Sadruddin Hossain and 'friendly fire?' Remember, as a Pakistan Air Force (PAF) pilot he was shot-down by 'friendly fire' in the 1965 India-Pakistan war by the Pakistanis, and now by the Indian Air Force?! What are the statistical chances of that happening to the same person and survive?! He must have the 'miracle gene' as he was unharmed but his chauffer had his leg blown off which had to be amputated.

That, fate has been very kind to him is bolstered by another miracle. In late October, he and the Sector Commander Wing Cmdr. Bashar were visiting the frontline areas out in the open. These Air force folks like open skies, and they probably thought they would have a clear view of the enemy position when suddenly 'boom'. The Pakistani military had an even clearer sight of them! An artillery shell from the enemy position landed a few meters from where they were standing. Most fortunately it was a dud, the shell did *not* explode and they survived to tell the story!

Confession of a Terrorist!
Chapter 7   Dream Come True

Two days after we had advanced to, and set-up our hospital in Thakurgaon, to our hilarity we hear from the Pakistan-controlled radio that the Pakistan Army was "gallantly fighting the 'Indian infiltrators' north of Thakurgaon and beating them back!" In reality they were about 40 km southeast in Saidpur trying to defend that town which had a very large Urdu-speaking Bihari population whose allegiance was to Pakistani rulers, naturally! By this time we became immune to the Pakistani propaganda machines' lies and disinformation; we were entertained as there was not much else to keep us amused. It is said that the first casualty of the war is truth; in this war that started on 25th March 1971, truth was not the first, it took a distant second place after countless millions of innocent Bengalis were slaughtered.

Mr. Sirkar's Thakurgaon Visit

On behalf of my fellow Freedom Fighters I was trying to find a way to express our deep gratitude to Mr. Sirkar for his generous support of our hospital. A couple of days after we established a secure and safe place in Thakurgaon I had gone to Shiliguri and gave him the news. He too was confused by the conflicting reports about the status of the

Confession of a Terrorist!
Chapter 7   Dream Come True

fighting – the allied forces of India and the People's Republic of Bangladesh claiming victories while the Pakistani propaganda machinery declaring their own version of triumph, and in Bengali. But he had a real-life proof in front of him. Excitedly he said that he wanted to visit Thakurgaon. I felt honored and gratified that under the circumstances this was the least I could do, to host him in a free [part of] Bangladesh that was liberated by our gallant Freedom Fighters of the *Mukti Bahini*. He immediately asked his driver to get ready and followed us in his vehicle – a long stretch white sports utility vehicle with big Red Cross insignias on the roof, both sides and the rear door; a vehicle that was loaded with all the necessary medical supplies that he could provide. I wondered how he justified these medical supplies in official documents!

In Thakurgaon he immediately went to see our wounded Freedom Fighters in the small house that served as a hospital. The young men were in bed with their brilliantly colored blankets, courtesy of Mr. Sirkar. He was pleased to see that his gifts were being used properly. No sooner I had arrived back in Thakurgaon I had asked our cook to get a *Rui* (carp) for our honored guest. And of course, he made *Muro Ghonto*[4] and other delicacies which Mr. Sirkar enjoyed very much. After the meal, he was telling me that a Sub-Sector commander in Rongpur area, also an Air Force officer had recently visited his office in Shiliguri. The commander came to know that we received the blankets from Mr. Sirkar and so he requested some for his soldiers too. Of course Mr. Sirkar generously gave away a few dozens of them. Several days later, I came to learn that a number of foreign-made beautiful blankets of vibrant color were available in the local market in Rongpur area!

...And Bivishon[5] in my Nightmare

Just so that you are still aware of the fact that the rest of the Bangladesh has not been liberated yet,

---

[4] *Muro Ghonto* is a slowly cooked dish featuring the head of carp and lentils and/or rice with some appropriate spices prepared for special celebratory occasion or for honored guests.

[5] According to Hindu mythology in *Ramayana*, Ravon of Lanka abducted Lord Ram's wife Sita. Ravan's youngest brother Bivishon not only disapproved the abduction, but also the call for a war. Bivishon was expelled from the royal court with indignity. So in the ensuing war with Lord Ram, Bivishon joined with Ram against his brother and gave valuable logistical information. Hence the infamous saying *"Ghorer Shotru Bivishon"* meaning Bivishon is the enemy in your own house or your brother is your adversary.
 http://www.sacred-texts.com/hin/dutt/rama09.htm

Confession of a Terrorist!
Chapter 7   Dream Come True

on or around 1st December, Daliah and I were coming back from Shiliguri late at night; it was around 23:00 Hr. or so; most of the villagers are fast asleep; the war is behind them, actually in front of them geographically speaking; the front line has moved south of the Thakurgaon and near Saidpur. Panchagarh has been liberated hardly 4-5 days prior. Since the combat zone was also away from me, I had some time for rest and recreation. We had gone to Shiliguri. Mr. Sirkar had his summer house in Darjeeling. He had asked me whether I have had the chance to visit Darjeeling. I told him about my failed attempt:

2nd Lt Matin and I had gone to the Base Hospital at the Indian Air Force base in Baghdogra at the foothills of the Himalaya to pick up one of our Freedom Fighters who was badly wounded and needed treatment and care that I could not provide. He was to be released that day. We went around 10:00 Hrs. to bring him back to Bangladesh; but he was not discharged by then; we were told to come back at 14:00 Hrs. instead. Matin and I were returning to Shiliguri and were wondering what we could do to kill time. Noxalbari[6] was about 10 km to the west;

---

[6] Noxalbari (also spelled as Naxalbari) is the name of the village in Darjeeling district where armed struggle by the Communists in West Bengal took place. On 25 May 1967 a poor farmer was

Confession of a Terrorist!
Chapter 7   Dream Come True

as famous or notorious place depending on one's point of view and political inclination, Matin was not keen on going there. Then suddenly I saw the road-sign for Darjeeling about 60 km or so. "How about that?" It did not take even a second for him to assent. We figured at 70-80 km/h we could be there in an hour or less, have lunch and be back by 14:00 Hrs. to pick up our patient. We told the driver to head for Darjeeling. We slowly started to ascend the Himalayan Mountain. The road was winding to put it very mildly, the bends were extremely sharp and going very steeply higher and higher in the mountain hugging the mountainside. These curves make those amongst the hills in Tripura like children's playground. At about 1,000 m elevation our driver got frightened as he could see how steep the mountain was and how deep the fall could be; that's when I took over the wheels. He literally took the back seat and was shivering in panic. We had

---

attacked over a land dispute. Ultra-leftist Maoist disguised as farmers retaliated by attacking the landlords under the leadership of Charu Mazumdar and Kanu Shannyal. The followers known as Noxalites (also called terrorists) had subsequently formed the Communist Party of India Marxist-Leninist (CPI ML). The Noxalite (or Naxalite) movement became immensely popular amongst students, for some inexplicable reason the brightest (!) not just in West Bengal but also in other parts of India and East Bengal. As of 2009 Noxalites are active in approximately 220 districts in 20 states of India that is 40% of total Indian Territory. (http://en.wikipedia.org/wiki/Naxalite).

passed Ghum, the then highest railway station in the world and on to Karsiyang, hardly 35 km or so; it took us almost 2 hours! Not that the road was bad, it wasn't; the pavement was excellent, it was just too zigzag and the risks were much too high for me to drive any faster; the local drivers were whizzing past me though!.

At that elevation of over 2,000 m Karsiyang was pretty cold and we were not prepared for it. Down at the foothills in the plains it was a bit nippy but not freezing cold. But here it was freezing! All three of us started to shiver; perhaps it was our imagination, the locals were looking at us somewhat curiously as we were scantily dressed. But they were discreet; they probably see many novices like us all the time. Karsiyang was well-known to me because of the radio station that played all my favorite songs. I was thrilled to be in there. However, my excitement did not stop the shivering though. We spotted a store selling *Mou Mou* a hot steamy soup that looked mouthwatering. It was a clear soup with some very mild local spices and dumpling; hot and delicious, and it made us warm. We soon left for Baghdogra to pick up our patient at 14:00 Hrs., knowing that it will take us that long.

Confession of a Terrorist!
Chapter 7 Dream Come True

Hearing this story Mr. Sirkar decided to take us there. His driver was a local young man in his midthirties; he has been doing this trip thousands of times; clearly, he knows each and every curve of the road. He was driving fast, a lot faster than I was, but very careful. We were in Darjeeling in no time, 40 minutes may be. I had heard about Darjeeling a lot and always wanted to go there. At an average elevation of over 2,000 m above the sea level Darjeeling is very clean and picturesque. The small houses and shops have a distinct architecture that I had not seen in the plains; they are especially designed for snowfall. They almost looked like toy houses. The city was very lively, there was a festive atmosphere in town; I asked Mr. Sirkar as to what festival was on, he said that that's the way it always is in Darjeeling. We had nice lunch at his house, walked around town, did some shopping, window shopping that is.

By the time we came back from Darjeeling to Shiliguri it was late, about 23:00 Hrs. The road from Shiliguri on to Thakurgaon had no traffic except for our jeep. It was pitch-dark. About 3 or 4 km inside the Bangladesh border out of nowhere I see a caravan of bullock-drawn carts heading north towards the Indian border. I slowed down. There were a lot of carts, after about 20 I lost the count.

Confession of a Terrorist!
Chapter 7   Dream Come True

Normally they have a small lamp at the bottom of the cart for oncoming traffic to see; these had none, even if they did, the lamps were out. Hmm; what's going on? The carts were all covered; since it was pitch dark we couldn't see the cargo anyway. At the end of the caravan was a jeep. I slowed almost to a halt, so did the other jeep. A man with moustache and long hair whom I recognized as the elected local member of the parliament (name withheld) jumped off the jeep. He recognized me immediately and was startled as if he saw a ghost! I had suspected that he was probably involved with the caravan and its cargo. At the middle of nowhere Daliah and I were the only two people; he on the other hand had another male companion and 20+ men on the carts. Everything has its time and place including heroism; I had decided that that was not the time to confront him, as a dead hero is not what I wanted to be. I drove off to come back to Thakurgaon where I told Mrs. Shirin Bashar about the incidence. She was not surprised as she had always suspected this; she had a hunch or woman's intuittion that the gentleman in question was a shady character. The next morning I came to know that the sugar mill of Panchagarh had been 'looted' the night before! What a coincidence!

We have a common tendency to find scapegoats to blame others for our own shortcoming. First we laid all the blames on the British for slicing up or partitioning of India, but rarely do we reflect on what our roles as Indians had in that. The Bengalis in East Bengal, now Bangladesh alternatively blame Pakistan and India, and sometimes simultaneously blame them both! But, what about us? Are we without flaw? Don't we have any responsibility? We started to loot and smuggle even before the war was over! I recalled one of the great lessons from Chairman Mao Zedong's Red Book about the importance of self-criticism; our Bengali nation could use a heavy dose of self-criticism; see what *we* are doing wrong and how *we* are hurting ourselves.

Free at Last!

By the 6th or 7th December, 1971 the armed conflict between the Bangladesh Liberation Army and Pakistan Army in our Sector had essentially ended with the advancing Indian Army taking over and the Pakistani Army 'gallantly' retreating. The war was far away from us now and we had this absolute confidence that victory is looming; this is the beginning of the end of East Pakistan at last. There were no more combat-injuries of our Freedom Fighters; they would have minor problems such as common cold, gastrointestinal disorders etc. and that too were on the wane. Furthermore, the hospital in Thakurgaon was well staffed and could adequately provide for all our needs. We could now relax and get some much needed recreation.

Daliah and I went to Shiliguri; where else to go? There we went shopping, I bought a nice sari for my wife and then we went to a Chinese restaurant. I had not had Chinese food for a long time, for that matter a nice meal except for the rare ones in Agartala at Dr. Roy Choudhury's house, one day in Darjeeling when I went with Mr. Sirkar to Darjeeling and in Murshidabad at Daliah's uncles' house. The meals we were having of late with the Bashar family were of course great. Those days, I was very fond of Chinese food; besides the typical Bengali dishes, that was the only exotic cuisine we had in East Pakistan. As a medical student, I was relatively wealthy; I was awarded a few scholarships and I lived in my parents' house. So, I had very little expenses. Like most of my friends, in high school days I used to collect stamps; one day I gave away all of mine to a friend as gift; so I wasn't spending money on that either. Besides that, I had a motorcycle for my transportation. The motorcycle was

Confession of a Terrorist!
Chapter 7   Dream Come True

fuel-efficient and the petroleum was also inexpensive. The tuition in Dhaka Medical College was virtually nothing (about Taka 1,000/year = US$250 during those days) compared to that in the USA ($20,000-$60,000); even that was waived for me – courtesy of one of the scholarships. Thus, I was relatively wealthy independently in my childhood and college days; I owe my motherland an eternal debt of gratitude for not just giving me free medical education but virtually paying me to become a physician and allowing me enough buying power.

I was a bit weird even as a child. At about the age of 8 while in Class IV, I had earned my very first money of about 9 Taka (approximately US$ 2.00 then) by winning the contest for naming the Prince bicycle[7]; all I wanted was to buy the famous sleek-looking Pilot pen from Japan at that time; not a toy, or a train set, but a pen! It was an expensive one, about 12 Taka; so I had to settle for the second best that I could afford the Indian Writer pen instead

---

[7] In or around 1955 a new bicycle, probably the only indigenous bicycle company was started in the then East Pakistan. They solicited the public for an attractive name and offered 100 Pakistani Rupees (or Taka in Bengali, 1 Taka = 16 Ana, 1 Ana = 4 Paisha). A total of 11 people including myself had proposed "Prince" as the name; so the award was divided equally amongst 11 resulting in each nominator receiving 9 Taka 1 Ana and some Paisha.

Confession of a Terrorist!
Chapter 7   Dream Come True

(That was another manner by which my father had instilled the value of spending within one's means in me – "cut your coat according the cloth you have" was his common uttering). Collecting pen has been my passion since childhood: Schaffer, Parker, Cross, Mont Blanc, Dunhill, *Caran d'Ache* etc., and all different colors and models, my not-so-good writing skills or penmanship notwithstanding. I also loved buying books. And still had money left; that would be going out to enjoy the various culinary delights in town and of course the exotic Chinese restaurants with my friends.

Neither did I stay long enough in Kolkata, nor was I in the mood to go on a bender on Chinese food there. This was the first time in nearly a year that I went to a Chinese restaurant. Why a year? Well, the uprising started from the late 1970's that precluded me to go out and have fun. It had been a somber period in our nation's history as well as in my life personally. This day, the Chinese food tasted like none I had before. It seemed that the Chinese cuisine adapts to the taste of the local populace. In East Bengal, it was moderately spicy; here in Shiliguri in the foothills of the Himalayas it was milder and had a tangy taste to it. Few months later when I went to a Chinese restaurant in Massachusetts in the United States, it was pretty bland to appease the taste of the local population. My cousins living in Paris wanted me to taste their version of Chinese food in the year 2005, it tasted almost French! Be that as it may, here in Shiliguri the Chinese food was not as greasy, the noodles were finer and the sauce quite scrumptious; this may have been the best Chinese food I ever had. I was as relaxed as one could be; my motherland is free, more or less that is, total freedom is guaranteed; heaven must feel like this.

"Give Me Blood and I Shall Get You Freedom"

Today, 16th December 1971 our motherland became completely free, the Pakistani military has surrendered unconditionally and we were celebrating. Wing Cmdr. Bashar as the Sector Commander was flying a small aircraft from Thakurgaon to Dhaka for the official surrender and celebration, our Sub-Sector Commander Sq. Ldr. Sadruddin Hossain was accompanying him. Knowing that my parents had no idea about my whereabouts let alone my wellbeing Wing Cmdr. Bashar most kindly offered Daliah and me to fly with him in his small plane. We were excited. And then all of a sudden: Boom – Boom – Boom!

Confession of a Terrorist!
Chapter 7   Dream Come True

We heard sounds of massive explosions in the distance. About 35 km south in the town of Dinajpur there was a tragic accident in our ammunition dump. It was in a school compound (Moharaja School) that temporarily served as the base for the advancing *Mukti Bahini*. The Freedom Fighters like the rest of the nation were jubilant; some were assigned to store the bombs and other ammunitions. In euphoria, they were less careful than they should have been in handling these dangerous explosives setting off a chain reaction that resulted in massive casualties. That there still is a crater at the time of composing this book in early to mid-2010 at the school compound is a testament to the immensity of the explosion.

Despite knowing that it was way beyond my capabilities to handle, I still could not shirk my responsibility; and I was not quite sure exactly what that was. Daliah and I rushed to Dinajpur. Oh what a pandemonium! The air was thick, smelled of spent explosives, burnt human flesh, and smoke. There was total chaos, dead and wounded Freedom Fighters everywhere. They were bleeding from large gaping wounds, their face and body blackened from the heat and scorch; they were lying on the ground; some walking in daze not knowing what to

Confession of a Terrorist!
Chapter 7 Dream Come True

do and where to go. Fortunately the medical team from the Indian Military that was nearby immediately was at the scene, long before I could be there and they were doing everything they could in the most efficient manner. It was fascinating observing their discipline, professionalism, teamwork and alacrity. They brought in their ambulances and mobile hospital unit fitted with laboratory. I had virtually nothing to do, but I wanted to help any which way I could. When I insisted I was told "no, there is nothing you could do." "How about blood, do you need any blood?" "We have enough of that;" of course they were prepared for the war; they just finished the powerful Pakistan Military without much effort, and they were all set for any eventuality; so they have a lot of unspent medical supplies and necessities. A paramedic a few meters away overheard our conversation, he hollered "Sir we are short of Type B+ blood." Guess what? That happened to be my blood type! Most elatedly I immediately laid down on the stretcher, another paramedical person struck a needle in my arm vein; I started to give all that was medically possible.

I recalled the graffiti in the walls in Dhaka before I left for Sonamura: my political hero since my childhood in his struggle against the British had called on our Indian nation to give blood – meaning

Confession of a Terrorist!
Chapter 7   Dream Come True

sacrifice; in return he said he will get us our freedom. Yes, *Netajee*, I'm delighted to report that finally I too now have the honor of responding to your call, I am privileged; I literally gave my blood even though it was not in combat as you meant and albeit on the day of our freedom! Nevertheless, I did it, no matter what the circumstance is or how little and how late it may have been! It went to someone who actually had been in combat though and suffered; and that makes me the happiest person on earth.

By the time we came back to Thakurgaon it was about 22:00 Hrs. Mrs. Shirin Bashar was very concerned and a bit distraught as she was worried about our safety. It was possible that there were pockets of Pakistani forces holed up for resisting the surrender, or there were Pakistani saboteurs etc. Needless to say, Wing Cmdr. Bashar had received all the information about the tragedy in Dinajpur, was assured that it was an accident and not related to the enemy operation. Being satisfied that the situation was under control, he had left for Dhaka albeit behind schedule due to the mishap.

CHAPTER 8

THE LONGEST MONTH

The Agony of Loss

ext comes the long wait; the country is independent, everyone is going home, all the Freedom Fighters are leaving, the regular army guys of *Mukti Bahini* were tough and disciplined; inasmuch as they wanted to go home to their family, they were planning on an orderly schedule of departure.

A couple of days later Wing Cmdr. Bashar returned from Dhaka. He told me that my father had met him at the then Intercontinental Hotel in Dhaka,

Confession of a Terrorist!
Chapter 8   Longest Month

Sheraton now-a-days. How did Dad know that I was in Sector 6, and Wing Cmdr. Bashar was my Commander? How did Dad find out that Wing Cmdr. Bashar was staying at the Intercontinental and managed to visit him precisely during that very narrow time-window? As busy as Wing Cmdr. Bashar was during those extraordinary moments in the history of our nation and in the midst of all the excitement, pomp and celebration with millions of people on the streets, a rendezvous would be tantamount to going through the eye of a needle. Dad, you never failed to surprise me, certainly not when it is related to showing your love for me and caring for me. I was relieved that my family members were fine and unharmed.

Not everyone was so fortunate however. One of the Freedom Fighters whom I had given emergency training to assist me came back from his home in Rajshahi; for there was no home left for him. He was totally devastated; owing to his participation in the Liberation War, his parents were brutally killed, their house burnt and his siblings are nowhere to be found; no one knew about their whereabouts. Having no place to go and no shoulder to cry on, he decided to come back to the place that has been his home on the run for the last few months. We were the only relatives that he could find solace with.

Confession of a Terrorist!
Chapter 8   Longest Month

The Bashar Family

Life in Thakurgaon was going on peacefully for us. Daliah and I stayed in the same house with the Bashar family. Wing Cmdr. Bashar had moved to Thakurgaon, the family is complete and happy. This was a large government Rest-House that used to be for the Engineers (the Engineers had all the luxury and fun, no wonder they were the most desirable of the bridegrooms!). There were several bedrooms with attached bathrooms that had Western-style commodes and other fixtures, a large living room, kitchen, dining room and servants' quarter. The compound was large with some flowering plants. All in all, it was a rather luxurious accommodation. We were eating well; besides eating and sleeping there was very little to do; the town was recovering from the devastation of the war and most of the Freedom Fighters were gone or on their way back home. I was rapidly gaining the weight that I had lost in Sector 2!

Mrs. Shirin Bashar had already adopted us as members of her family back in Tetulia when we first arrived. She stayed back there with Shompa and Ika till Thakurgaon was liberated when she moved here. By this time she became my elder,

Confession of a Terrorist!
Chapter 8   Longest Month

wiser sister. Being the oldest child in my family, I did not have the benefit of an older sibling who would guide me or advise me. I had some older cousins but they were not available. Mrs. Shirin Bashar filled that void in me and gave me the love and affection, and the wisdom of an older sibling. I had many long and very educational discussions with her about politics, life, society etc. She was an extremely intelligent and wise person. One of the things I liked about her most was her forthrightness. She was unpretentious, yet polite and courteous but firm. She was as kind as she was strict. Their two daughters Shompa and Ika were the sweetest of all the kids. Shompa the eldest was tall and slim, she reminded me of my childhood as that's how I was. During this period Shompa had lost her two front teeth and looked particularly cute. Shompa's physical appearance was more like her mother's. Ika was a bit short with dark and shiny curly hair; the hair seemed to have come from her father's side. She demonstrated a strong personality even at the tender age of 4-5. They were a joy to be with.

One day Wing Cmdr. Bashar decided to take the family to Darjeeling for a much needed rest and recreation. As magnanimous as he was, he took Daliah and me in the tow. It was a treat! We arrived at the palatial Oberoi Mount Everest Hotel a little

Confession of a Terrorist!
Chapter 8   Longest Month

after dusk, probably around 19:00 Hrs. Built in 1914 and located on Gandhi Road it was the heritage landmark of Darjeeling that was initially run as Darjeeling Family Hotel by one Mr. Stephen. In 1950 it was leased to Mr. M.S. (Mohan Singh) Oberoi, the Indian hotelier giant who was originally from the part of Punjab that is now in Pakistan, for 100 years. The hotel had a grand entrance, the lobby was quite spacious and had very high ceiling. Wing Cmdr. Bashar rented two suites, one for him and his family, and the other for Daliah and me.

The suites were very spacious with high ceilings, thick stone walls and simply but elegantly decorated; they were impeccably clean. There were fireplaces in each room but for some reason no firewood and hence no fire; the rooms were a bit cold, but we slept quite comfortably tucked under the plush duvet. We were told that the Tiger Hill area was a must-see to view the spectacular sunrise over Mount Kanchonjonga range. For that, one has to get up at 04:00 to make it in time for the sunrise; or it's too late. Inasmuch as we wanted to enjoy this magnificence, we were much too tired and/or lazy to wake up that early in the morning. After all, considering the hardship we had gone through including sleeping on *hogla* mats with the mosquito militia, boots as pillows during the months prior and

Confession of a Terrorist!
Chapter 8   Longest Month

being on the run after the fleeing Pakistani military; and now having immersed ourselves in this great luxury, we simply could not or did not get up. As you can imagine, it was very difficult to leave that comfort, we did not want it to end so soon; we wanted to cling to that as long as we could. So the Tiger Hill sunrise had to wait for another time. Instead, we got up way past 10:00 Hrs, had a leisurely breakfast and afterwards went strolling, sightseeing and window-shopping in Darjeeling. And the best of all, Wing Cmdr. Bashar paid for all of our suite, sumptuous meals and all other incidental expenses; what a kindhearted and generous person. He had to; I did not have any money!

During one of these days, Wing Cmdr. Bashar was relaxed enough to tell me his story of joining the *Mukti Bahini*. He was in command of a squadron of Pakistan Air Force in Dhaka. While our Prime Minister-elect Sheikh Mujibur Rahman was engaged in rather futile negotiations with the Pakistani authorities, Wing Cmdr. Basher could see that under the guise of negotiations the Pakistanis were strengthening their troops in the East. Being alarmed, he and his senior officer Group Captain Khondokar tried to convey the message to Sheikh Mujibur Rahman and other high ranking politicians. Gr. Capt. Khondokar was the senior-most Bengali

Confession of a Terrorist!
Chapter 8   Longest Month

Air Force officer in Dhaka and therefore was in a position to command the loyalty of the Bengali Air Force personnel. Since Wing Cmdr. Bashar was in command of the radar station at Dhaka airport that is critical for the landing of the planes bringing new troops from Pakistan every night and the flight of the air force fighter/bomber planes under his and Gr. Capt. Khondokar's leadership they could blockade the airport, choking off Pakistani military's supply line; in those days, there was only a squadron (12-24 aircrafts) of fighter jets in Dhaka.

That the Pakistan Central government did not care about East Pakistan was evident here again by the meager one squadron of ageing F86 Sabre Jets from the Korean War era for the entire province. I suppose that either they never expected India to seriously fight in the eastern front or simply surrender in the event of an all-out air-strike by India! Be that as it may, Sheikh Mujibur Rahman and his advisers rebuffed at that idea. Getting the cold shoulder from the politicians and having committed treason, an offence tried by court-martial most likely facing the firing squad, he and Gr. Capt. Khondokar had no choice but to defect and join the Resistance; they arrived in Sonamura in Sector 2 in mid-May. Like me and many others, they too were the guests in the 'Sonamura Sheraton at the river-

Confession of a Terrorist!
Chapter 8   Longest Month

front'! Of note, he did not tell me this story when we first met, or the many other occasions since then, but only at the end of our struggle; for he did not want to belittle the Prime Minister or the other politicians, especially when we're in the midst of our Liberation War. What a contrast with Lt. Col. Khaled Mosharraf of Sector 2 who was rather openly criticizing the government-in-exile and his Commander-in-Chief and worse, planning a *coup d'état* back in June, the early days of our resistance!

One of my uncles, not related by blood, but who hailed from the same village as my Dad, Ismail *Kaka*[1] used to live in Patgram, a small town in the northern part of Rongpur district where he owned a bookstore and a pharmacy. Ismail *Kaka* was a high school student in Kurmitola in Dhaka not far from where the current day Hazrat Shahjalal (formerly Zia) International Airport is [I hope that the politicians stop changing the names, it's getting hard to keep up!]. My Dad, one of his brothers, one

---

[1] *Kaka* (or more affectionately *Kaku*) refers to father's younger brother; the older brother is called *Jetha*, mother's brothers are *Mama* irrespective of their position in relation to mother but there are terms to be specific as well. In Bengali culture, as in many other Asian and some European cultures, it is not only polite but also the norm to address parents' male friends as uncles – *Kaka* or *Jetha* depending on their age and *Mama* to mother's male friends.

Confession of a Terrorist!
Chapter 8 Longest Month

of my mother's brothers and I lived there till 1953. In 1952 Ismail *Kaka* was in Class X and about to take his matriculation examination when I was little over 3. There was police shooting resulting in deaths of unarmed students who were demanding for Bengali to be our national language on 21st February.

I distinctly recall boarding the trains at Kurmitola station that were leaving Dhaka and going north with him to look for the then Chief Minister Mr. Nurul Amin chanting "*Rashtro vasha Bangla Chai, Nurul Aminer Kolla Chai* or *Nurul Aminer Rockto chai*" (We want Bengali to be our state language and down with Nurul Amin etc.) in the stopped train, in the event that Mr. Nurul Amin might be fleeing Dhaka on the only escape route. It was during Mr. Nurul Amin's tenure as Chief Minister that the Pakistan Government reiterated the position that Bengali the language of the over-whelming majority of East Pakistanis as well as of the majority of Pakistanis as a whole, was not to be considered a national language. Bengali nationalists consider his behaviors and position on the issue as treachery as he was a Bengali himself. In my childhood days I looked up to Ismail *Kaka*[2] for

---

[2] Though Ismail *Kaka* was a Moslem and would be called Ismail *Chacha* by many Bengali Moslems now-a-days, my family had

Confession of a Terrorist!
Chapter 8   Longest Month

he was affectionate, a serious student yet one who also cared about our culture and an intellectual. I had not seen him for ages. So here in Patgram, the Command Head-Quarter for Sector 6, I decided to look him up. Patgram appeared like a ghost town. When we arrived there at midday, all the stores were closed; there was not a single person to be found on the street. It looked like all the citizens have left town perhaps in anticipation of the atrocities associated with war and victorious armies etc.; understandably so as not even a week has passed since the Liberation. I found the book store

---

resisted the fanatic total "Islamization" by not shedding off all of the true and original Bengali culture. In my grandparents' village the Hindus and Moslems lived very close to each other. Perhaps owing to this total harmony the Moslems in that area, especially my parents' family did not feel the urge to make much distinction from their Hindu neighbors with whom they enjoyed a normal relationship (my 'cousin' Girendra was a Hindu and his mother was my aunt though not blood related). They did everything together except praying to different higher authorities at different times. While non-Muslims are prohibited from entering the mosques for fear of 'desecration,' like the Christian churches, the Hindu temples are open to all. Furthermore, the Muslim Eid festivals are restricted to mass prayer followed by feasting. If it was not for the mouth-watering varieties of the food and visiting relatives, friends and neighbors, I found them rather humdrum. In contrast the Hindu Puja festivals are a lot of fun – the music, the songs, the dance, the food, the plays, poetry recitations, *Jatra* (operatic plays), other cultural activities and the carnival render them very festive. And of course there were a lot of pretty girls! Thus in my childhood I never missed a Puja festival.

and the pharmacy that he owned or used to own; were closed too. We then went to Holdibari in Jalpaiguri district of West Bengal, India. The HeadQuarter in Patgram was not far from the Holdibari train station which has not been operating for quite some time. The train line is one of the few that connects India to Bangladesh; in here it connects Jolpaiguri, Shiliguri to the north in India and Saidpur to the south in Bangladesh. The rails on the track were rusted, there has not been any train running on those for a long time. Jolpaiguri was a nice little town, very clean and well laid out, the houses were spread out with nice yards that had lots of flowering plants, there were plenty of tall trees; Sq. Ldr. Sadruddin knew of a journalist who was an editor of the local news-paper; we went to his house and enjoyed their cordial hospitality.

Surrendering the Arms

Following the liberation of Thakurgaon, Sq. Ldr. Sadruddin's job was essentially finished. Now he has the responsibility of collecting the firearms from the Freedom Fighters and issuing them with documentations (certificates that were printed in Shiliguri) of their service to the nation. Sq. Ldr. Sadruddin was successful in collecting at least 90%

of the firearms that was issued to the Freedom Fighters! While that is a remarkable achievement compared to other Sub-Sectors, the fact that 10% arms were uncollected is hardly a cause for celebration.

The submachine gun that I was assigned to was no longer needed, at least not for protecting ourselves from the Pakistani enemy. To my utter dismay, yet not unexpectedly, the law and order situation had become terrible; there were news of looting, mugging, robberies etc. There were lots of guns out there (10% that were not returned, and that's no small number!). Each Freedom Fighter had a gun, usually a submachine gun; many Freedom Fighters became disgruntled, angry and depressed; some lost their parents, others lost siblings or friends or all. Then there were the Bengali religious fanatics and Bihari chums of Pakistan military - the *Razakars, Al-Bodor* and *Al-Shams* who had inflicted a lot of the atrocities. It was time for revenge! And revenge there was. In the process, there was near anarchy. Courtesy of the Pakistan military, the *Razakars, Al-Bodor* and *Al-Shams* militia had arms too. Then there were some bad elements within the Freedom Fighters. Some became greedy; with the power of having guns and ammunitions some embarked on looting and other antisocial and criminal activities. Essentially it was not a safe period. I was in a dilemma whether to surrender my arms or not.

What harm could possibly happen to me? I did not have any money or any other material wealth that could be useful to a potential robber. To the best of my knowledge and perhaps illusion, I did not have any enemy who would like to take revenge on me; the only enemies I had are behind the bars, safe under the watchful guard of the Indian Military. So why do I need a gun for? Will I shoot a former Freedom Fighter who is coming to rob me? He may take whatever little I have from me; he must have a compelling reason to do so. But I am not going to shoot him. All things considered I decided to return my submachine gun to the Subedar in charge.

My Heroes
The Pundit

"Where are you from?"
-Komolpur.
[A pause from the questioner]
"Who is your father?"
-Dr. Zainul Abedin

Confession of a Terrorist!
Chapter 8   **Longest Month**

Hmmm [A *l-o-n-g-e-r* pause from the questioner, he couldn't recognize the good doctor]
"Who is your grandfather?"
-Abdul Majid Pondith (Pundit)
"Ah! So, you are the Pondith's grandson! Why didn't you say that to begin with?! And how is Pondith shaheb? [The questioner's voice crackling with adulation]"

I was about 6 or 7 years of age, walking through the meadows from my father's village in Laksham, Comilla to my mother's in Chatkhil, Noakhali; about 6 km away; I met the farmer about half way. In this very meadow, coincidentally at or around this spot, I received one of my first lessons in civic duty from by Dad. The farmers in the 1950's were barefoot. Some of them would be hauling the branches of a special thorny tree (*Mandar gaach*) that would serve as the natural version of barbed-wire fence; invariably twigs with thorns would be littered on the path. My dad would pick those up and throw them on the side; he reminded me that unlike us, the poor farmers did not have shoes; it was our duty to make sure that they are not hurt! Little did the farmer who did not recognize my father know it was my dad who was looking after his wellbeing!

Confession of a Terrorist!
Chapter 8   Longest Month

My parents and I had moved to Dhaka when I was about 3 and have lived there till 1971. Both my parents were very close to their parents and we would visit them every 3 months or so. My dad revered his father; Dad felt that my grandfather was the wisest man on earth, I too felt the same way; before making any major decision, Dad would always consult with my grandfather. Even though Dad and I were extremely close I did not know whether he had a hero; if there was one, it must have been granddad. But my grandfather was surely my hero, the first one and continues to enjoy that stature being at the top of the list.

At about 180 cm Grandpa was tall, relatively speaking that is, for average Bengali. And slim. He stood straight without even any suggestion of a hunch still at 90. He walked for kilometers after kilometers, about 10 km only two days before his final rest. He was always calm and cool; I never saw him angry except when I made him, deliberately that is! I used to visit him and Grandma often, or as often as I could; it was a long trip those days, taking the whole day to travel about 160 km from Dhaka. I would tell Grandpa that I was going to return to my parents in Dhaka on a certain day. Very seriously he would look up the almanac, and with an even more serious face tell me "...Oh that's

Confession of a Terrorist!
Chapter 8   Longest Month

not a good day to travel." To prove that I am not superstitious, I would insist on traveling the day he would make up to be a bad one; he would be so mad! Of course I knew that he only wanted me to be with him a few days more; his plan backfired; can you blame him for being annoyed?

Grandpa was a farmer with not much education; so why was he called Pondith (pundit) and why is he my hero? Because he may have been a farmer and/or illiterate does not mean he was unintelligent; as a matter of fact it was not just in my mind, but also to the villagers within 5+ km radius, a very wise man. In the event of a dispute the villagers did not go to the court or the police, they called Pondith shaheb (The Pundit). On two or three occasions, I had accompanied this Pondith shaheb to his mediation sessions. Grandpa would go on fact-finding mission on his own before the mediations; he would investigate the root cause(s) of the disagreement, and find a fair and equitable solution *a priori*. The mediation sessions would be scheduled for evening after supper. Grandpa would just sit there and let the opposing parties talk, small talk, jokes, anything. The discussions were amicable even though the disputes may have been very contentious. Most of the villagers are farmers who work very hard and long hours during the day, all day;

Confession of a Terrorist!
Chapter 8   Longest Month

naturally they would be tired and sleepy, especially after supper. Pretty soon they would be running out of subjects, serious or otherwise and would be drowsy; that's when grandpa would take charge. He would be asking the parties to tell in two or three sentences what their complaint and/or problems were; grandpa was a man of action and not talks. Then without any discussion he would render his solution which he had already thought of very carefully long beforehand. Both the disputing parties would be stunned and exultant as it was a very just and reasonable solution; they would be ready to kiss his hand! For a 4-5 year old child to witness such adulation for his grandfather was reason enough to make him my very first hero.

Later in my childhood I was told by my mother (Dad never talked about it lest it appears that he's bragging about his father!) that only due to him, the minority Hindu population in our village and in the neighboring ones within a few kilometers was absolutely unharmed during the Hindu-Muslim riots around the time of Indian-Pakistani independence (our area had seen one of the worst riots, enough to make Mahatma Gandhi come to Jayag in adjacent district of Noakhali on 29 January 1947, about 5 km to the south and stay for four months, to try pacifying the mobs). They were safe not be-

Confession of a Terrorist!
Chapter 8   Longest Month

cause Grandpa was a political leader, a "strongman" or a mafia-boss type of a person; it was out of the deep respect he commanded in the area. I'm sure Mahatma Gandhi's four month-long stay also had something to do with it (Gandhi-*jee* did not come to our village, but he had been to my mom's in Noakhali, an event she adoringly recollects). That is another great reason why Grandpa continues to enjoy that stature high up in my mind and heart. I suppose being encouraged by such adulation Grandpa tried his luck in local politics to be Chairman of the Union Council equivalent to a County Executive in the early 1950's. On the Election Day I saw columns of women, Hindus in white sari and black burka-clad Muslims looking like the "March of the Penguins" diagonally crossing the meadows to go to the polling stations. While all the able bodied men and women of Hindu faith walked several kilometers to vote for him *en masse*, he lost narrowly for not getting enough votes from the majority Muslim population!

While out of respect for him, they had restrained themselves in not hurting their neighbors in the 1940's, they did not want Grandpa's political legitimacy to hold them back from subsequent malevolent behavior, perhaps. Sadly, we have witnessed the aftermath of those actions in the form of

Confession of a Terrorist!
Chapter 8   Longest Month

steady exodus of the Hindu population not just from our community but from the rest of East Bengal (East Pakistan by then). Alas, as great a man as he was, that Grandpa could not stop.

He was no less of a hero on personal matters too. He would always address grandma in the most polite and affectionate terms yet respectful. I know it's hard to comprehend that now-a-days, but that's the way he was. And I had never seen or heard my grandparents argue over anything! His leading by example may have profoundly affected my parents too; I had not seen them arguing in the 22 years that I lived with them! Now, that does not mean they did not have disagreement; on the contrary they did not agree on a few things but they discussed and resolved in manners that could not be any more civil. My grandma and my mom must take a lot of credit for that too. Neither the men nor the women seemed to have given the other partners any reason to make them upset; but that does not mean they were sissies or walkovers either! Aside from their love for each other, that mutual respect on a day-to-day basis was probably the more important foundation for their absolutely wonderful relationship.

Confession of a Terrorist!
Chapter 8   Longest Month

In 2008, I went to pay my respect to one of the rare surviving nonagenarians in our neighboring village of Monipur, about 2 km from ours. He, a Hindu gentleman fondly recalled grandpa's role in the community; I received the VIP treatment just because I was his grandson!

Interestingly, while I was in Class VI, sardonically my Technical High School (later Intermediate Technical College and currently Government Science College) classmate Danial Islam (retired as a Brigadier in the Army) used to call me Pundit. I have no idea why all of a sudden, he started to address me that way, but I did not dare tell him that while I might not have been a pundit, I was however the Pundit's grandson!

My inborn admiration for brilliant creative people who also have other strong extracurricular attributes, most importantly social conscience and social responsibility made me naturally attracted to the great Chemist Linus Pauling. He became my scientist-hero not just because of his seminal contributions in science, but also to world peace; he was not just an outstanding scientist, but a superb human being too. He was only one of the four individuals who received multiple Nobel Prizes and considered one of the most influential scientists of the 20th

Century. He is one of only two people to have been awarded a Nobel Prize in two different fields (the Chemistry and Peace prizes)[3], and the only person to have been awarded each of his prizes without sharing it with another recipient! His research on X-ray crystallography of the DNA structure was used by James Watson, Francis Crick, Maurice Wilkins and Rosalind Franklin to arrive at the structure of DNA double helix.

Dr. Pauling's peace activism for banning aboveground nuclear testing following Second World War earned him the Nobel Peace Prize but may have cost him another (the third!) Nobel Prize, in Chemistry. While Dr. Pauling was independently working on the DNA structure, he was prevented from attending a crucial conference in UK because the US Department of State had withheld his passport on the suspicion that he had Communist sympathies; a terrorist?! To me, he embodies the ideal scientist, a super brilliant man with social conscience; the former attribute he was born with - which I was not, but I certainly can strive to develop, emulate and nurture the moral sense that he had.

---

[3] The other scientist to have received the Nobel Prizes in two different fields was Marie Curie: the Chemistry (1911) and Physics (1903) prizes.

Confession of a Terrorist!
Chapter 8   Longest Month

Netajee

In 1984 during the second of my many trips to Japan, I was conducting a month-long collaborative research at the National Cancer Center Research Institute in Tsukiji, Tokyo in the laboratory of Dr. Susumu Nishimura. Dr. Nishimura was in his late 60's and had worked with the Nobel Laureate Dr. Hare Govind Khorana at the MIT (Massachusetts Institute of Technology) outside Boston; that's the closest I came in the world of "six degrees of separation" with a Nobel Laureate. Aside from being a brilliant scientist and a great human being, Dr. Nishimura was also politically very conscious. He was in his twenties during World War II and as soon as he came to know that I was a Bengali he asked me whether I knew of *Netajee*.

With Japanese financial, diplomatic, political, and military assistance *Netajee* formed the Azad Hind Government in exile. Dr. Nishimura recalled the many visits *Netajee* had in Japan and took me to an Indian restaurant in Ginza area in Tokyo; Indian cuisine was just becoming popular in Japan then. As I walked into this small 2x4 m dining room, I felt like I walked into a small museum for *Netajee*. The wall was full of photographs of *Netajee* and *Azad Hind Fauz* (literally meaning Free or

Confession of a Terrorist!
Chapter 8   Longest Month

Independent Indian Force, a.k.a. <u>I</u>ndian <u>N</u>ational <u>A</u>rmy or INA) with virtually no free space left. Then there were small statues and busts of *Netajee* that were on display. There were only 3 or 4 tables for dining; the rest of the space seems to have been taken up by *Netajee* paraphernalia. There were some pictures of the restaurant-owner in INA uniform; he was an Indian gentleman from Kerala, in his early seventies, and was most proud to tell me that he served in INA. For him *Netajee* was a demigod, like many other freedom-loving Indians. He was "preaching the choir!"

Around the time when I was in Class VI or VII, besides my grandpa, I found another hero: it was *Netajee* Shuvash Chandra Bose. His academic brilliance was a natural fascination for me; as a student he topped the list in the province-wide matriculation examination in Kolkata; what a feat! He was a fierce nationalist who wanted nothing short of total and immediate independence of India. His stealthy manners were the subject of folklores; his sudden and mysterious disappearance while under house-arrest by the British and reappearance in places like Kabul, Afghanistan and Berlin, Germany, in the midst of Second World War was mesmerizing to the masses. His radio broadcast from Berlin in German radio sent shock waves among

Confession of a Terrorist!
Chapter 8   Longest Month

the British and electrified the Indian masses. Realizing that *Netajee* was working on a grand strategy to free their motherland it boosted the morale of the Indians sky-high and gave fresh confidence to the other Indian revolutionaries[4].

His superman-like energy and valor was also legendary; while the war was being fought on the land, air and sea globally, he was traveling between Germany, Soviet Union, South Asia and Japan, many times in submarines and rubber dinghies! That he had the most profound influence on me than any other person in my life is reflected in my desire as a child to adopt his name!

I never understood why as a Bengali I had an Arabic name; true I was born in a Moslem family but what has a name - a proper noun has to do with the family's religion? Again, thanks to my dad's teaching of reading the newspapers, I was familiar with the life history of the first president of Indonesia Mr. Sukarno who was born Kusno Sosrodihardjo. Adding to the conundrum was the fact that he was a Moslem, but his name was Indonesian. Likewise, many other Indonesians that I read about including General Suharto were Muslims [of course there are members of other religious

---

[4] http://www.kamat.com/kalranga/itihas/bose.htm

Confession of a Terrorist!
Chapter 8   Longest Month

affiliations] with Indonesian names and none Arabic. The little education I had told me that a name - proper noun belongs to a language and Bengali was my mother-tongue. Why do Indonesians who are no less Muslims than the Bengalis can chose to have their Indonesian names, yet the Bengali Muslims must have Arabic names?! Wait a minute, there are Arab Christians too! So why having an Arabic name automatically makes one Muslim?! "Shuvash" besides being a very beautiful name meaning 'one who speaks well or eloquently' (and he was a great orator who energized his audiences), for me *Netajee* was an embodiment of the ultimate patriot. Oh how I had wished I was his namesake.

In July 1972 when I came to the United States, at Lawrence General Hospital, the hospital telephone- and paging-operator suggested that I change my name to Dr. Smith or something like that as they could not pronounce Dr. Shamsuddin. Notwithstanding the fact that I was not crazy about my Arabic name, my response was that they will have to learn to pronounce it; I decided to like my name henceforth!

Of course *Netajee's* demigod status was not amongst all Indians. There were some who were not comfortable with this alliance with the Germans

Confession of a Terrorist!
Chapter 8   Longest Month

and Japanese in order to fight the British. That the European colonial powers were fighting and annihilating each other was least of India's problem; it may even be a welcome event. Would the Germans, Italians, or French have been worse colonialists than the British? After all, India was dragged into the war by the British without even consulting our leaders, only to use Indian supplies for their war and men as cannon fodders, my dad included[5]. So for *Netajee* and his followers, it did not matter; "enemy of my enemy is my friend!" Not too long after the Second World War, Tip O'Neal, the Speaker of the House in the neo-colonialist power United States, as if to vindicate *Netajee* stated "all politics is local." Sure enough for India, locally the politics for 190 years has been to gain independence from the British.

And of course, Khudiram Bose is another of my political heroes; he threw the first bomb on the British thereby leading the way for subsequent struggle, armed or otherwise for the independence of India.

---

[5] Dad served in the British Indian Army during the Second World War in the Southeast Asian Theatre. He was an Instructor stationed in Java Indonesia and was in Singapore during the surrender of the Japanese.

Confession of a Terrorist!
Chapter 8   Longest Month

By now you must have guessed that Maj. Dr. Akhtar Ahmed is one of my heroes. Aside from his conventional display of heroic participation in the mutiny and providing medical aid while being in the line of fire, I was most impressed by his deep patriotism - unselfish and unquestionable; his ethics, manner, personality and ideals. That he is a real war-hero has been recognized by the Government of the Peoples' Republic of Bangladesh by awarding him *"Beer Protik"* (Exemplary Hero) after the liberation of the country. In this war, amongst so many heroes I found another one that has similar attributes as Maj. Akhtar as my hero; he is Wing Cmdr. Khademul Bashar, who subsequently became the Chief of Bangladesh Air Force. In many ways the two men are very similar; neither of them flaunted their patriotism or cashed-on on it. Wing Cmdr. Bashar's nonchalant demeanor masks the Royal Bengal tiger inside. Again, in my personal opinion he was as patriotic and dutiful as anyone could ever ask for. He was fair, serious yet fun-loving and always was in complete control of himself. It was not just pleasure, but great privilege and honor to be with him and his family, and serve my motherland under his command.

After the 6th or 7th December, when the Indian Military was directly engaging the Pakistanis, Wing

Confession of a Terrorist!
Chapter 8 Longest Month

Cmdr. Bashar could take a bit of much needed well deserved rest and relaxation. Daliah and I were in the Government Rest House in Thakurgaon with Mrs. Shirin Bashar, and Shompa and Ika. Around 9th or 10th December he arrived late at night, it must have been way past midnight, from his Head-Quarters. The next morning I saw an elaborate set of Hi-Fi stereo system taking up much of the wall on one side of the living room. Wing Cmdr. Bashar knew that we were dying out of curiosity. At breakfast table he told us the story: Since the Pakistan army was on the run, the local high ranking Indian Officers were already in the mood to relax and have fun; Wing Cmdr. Bashar was not left alone. They were playing poker, a game he does not play often, but on rare occasions when he does, he wins most of the time – I was told by his wife. This happened to be one of those usual – he won and won big. What to do with the bounty? By the time they finished the game it was already past 23:00 Hrs. the stores in Shiliguri were all closed. That did not matter. He had managed to bring the storekeeper from home, open the store and purchase the stereo set, spending the last Rupee he won. What an astute man!

A few days later, he came with a brown leather sac that was being heavily guarded by his Batman.

Confession of a Terrorist!
Chapter 8 Longest Month

Half-jokingly I asked whether it was full of money; he replied affirmatively. To that I asked whether it was again his gambling booty. "It is the salary money for the Freedom Fighters" was his answer to my astonishment. Seeing this look of disbelief in me he explained that since April or May the Government of India had been most generously paying regular salary to each enlisted Freedom Fighters (an estimated 120,000) and this was their salary for the month of December. Though my recollection of the salary structure may not be quite accurate, it was something like the following: About 75 Rupees for each Freedom Fighter at the lowest rank that included the volunteer Freedom Fighters and the lowest ranking sepoys (equivalent to a Private in US Army); the enlisted members of the *Mukti Bahini* in the rank of Habildar 100 Rupees, Subedar 150 Rupees and so on; Officers received higher amounts, again depending on the rank 2nd Lieutenant, Lieutenant, Captain, Major and Lt Col all received a graded salary. I recalled that in Sector 2 many Freedom Fighters had complained that they did not receive any money, and if some did it was occasionally. To that he simply stated that they were supposed to, and dropped the topic lest it appears as his finger-pointing his colleague. One cannot help but have a high regard for such manners and character. He is my hero. And so are those Freedom Fighters who have selflessly served our motherland.

I am ever so grateful to the Bashar family for their generosity and kindness. Following the liberation I stayed in touch with Bashar family through the mysterious death of Air Chief Khademul Bashar. In or around mid-1997 while in Baltimore, Maryland, I received a call from Ontoo, the third child and son of the Bashars. He came to USA and was in need of some financial help; unfortunately that was the time I was going through the termination of my 25 years of marriage (27 years of relationship) with Daliah and finance was one of the touchy matters. Knowing Daliah, she would not have consented to helping him. Having joint bank accounts and financial arrangements, to my utter regret ethically I could not unilaterally make any financial commitment to him either. Wing Cmdr. Bashar, I beg your forgiveness for my failure to reciprocate your generosity and kindness. But should there be a "second chance" I shall make every effort to rectify my failing.

Homecoming

Both Wing Cmdr. Bashar and Mrs. Bashar were concerned about the fact that Daliah and I had not

Confession of a Terrorist!
Chapter 8   Longest Month

seen our parents since the independence. It seemed that they were more concerned about it than we were. But Wing Cmdr. Bashar was very astute. He did not want to simply tell us to go. He took full responsibility for us. Only when he was confident that given the deteriorated law & order situation in the nascent country, that we could safely travel from the farthest place to Dhaka, he was willing to arrange for our transport.

Exactly a month after the Victory over Pakistan, on 16 January, 1972 he had his personal Command vehicle with the military insignia (to ward off any potential miscreants) along with not one, but two bodyguards armed with submachine guns and of course the driver, sent to me. He however given me very strict order that I was not to drive the vehicle at all. That may have been the wrong directive as I was a much better driver than the one who was assigned to us. He then personally handed me the certificate of my service in the sector as a R.M.O (Regimental Medical Officer) and sent me off.

Confession of a Terrorist!
Chapter 8   Longest Month

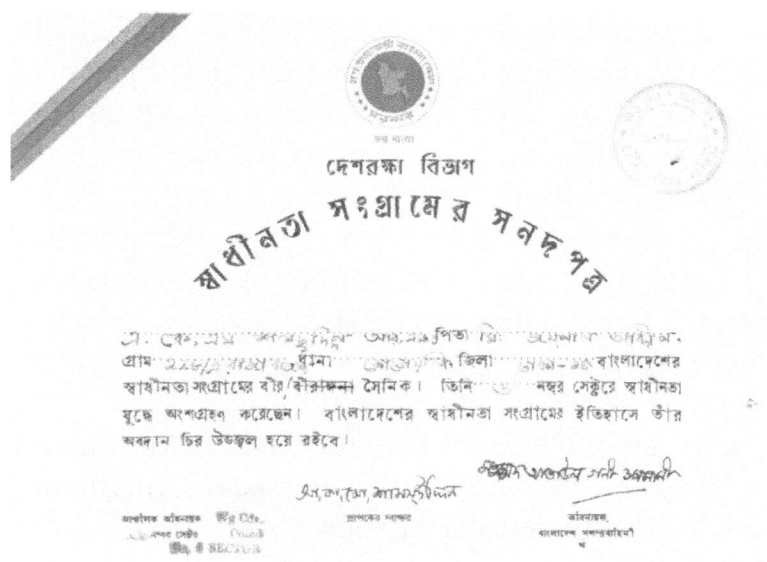

My Certificate from Sector 6

This was a long and arduous journey. Virtually all the bridges were blown off, at the beginning of our Resistance mostly by us – the *Mukti Bahini* to stop the Pakistan military, to harass them and engage them for ambushes; the few remaining were lately blown by the retreating Pakistan military so as to slow down the advancing Joint Forces of mostly Indian military accompanied by the Bangladesh Liberation Forces. The end result is that we had to take detours for almost all the bridges. Being winter, a dry season in Bangladesh, some of the

Confession of a Terrorist!
Chapter 8 — Longest Month

smaller shallow rivers and creeks were dry or low in tide; those we could cross; for others, we had to

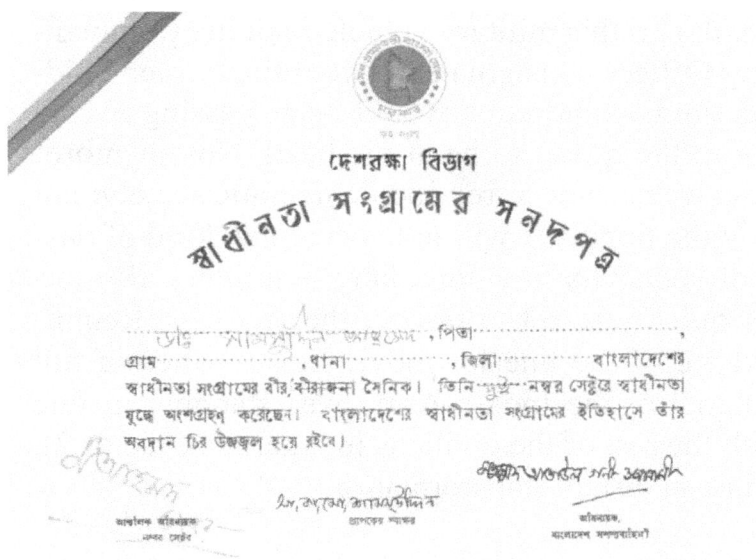

The certificate from Sector 2 was given to me after my return to Dhaka (with error in my name)

take ferries. In order to either cross the riverbed or get on to the ferry we had to negotiate the steep riverbanks. These off-track pathways were quite bumpy and due to the vertical slope quite dangerous. For the ferries, there were long lines of cars, trucks, buses etc. and the drivers did not want to waste a moment to lose their spot in the queue.

Confession of a Terrorist!
Chapter 8 Longest Month

I noted a change in the attitude of the common people. While prior to the liberation, the Pakistani military had the privilege and rights for priority; a month ago this military vehicle with the Commanding Officer's insignia and two military men holding submachine guns would be bypassing everyone in the queue to be at the head. Not anymore! Now we became a free and democratic society; not only the populace will not accept that kind of dastardly behavior anymore, but the military also rather quickly learnt to respect the civilians. Reminded me of the line for movie tickets where a full Colonel of the Indian Army was standing in line with the rest of the civilians in Agartala (Sector 2). What an instant transformation!

Thus, not to lose our place in the queue, despite the jerky and dangerous jaunt, we were asked to stay put in the jeep. One of the last such bridges that were blown was about 60 km south of Bogura, 50 or so km northwest of the main ferry crossing of River Jamuna at Shirajgonj. As we were approaching to get on the small makeshift ferry with very crude and improvised ramp (if it can be so called), again the driver insisted that we did not get off the jeep. However, this time instead of moving on to the ferry very slowly and carefully, he started to speed up for reason I never understood. I was in the "killer seat" – the passenger seat on the front, hit my forehead to the dash-board and before I knew I was bleeding profusely from a deep cut about 2 cm in length on my left eyebrow. Fortunately this being the Commanding Officer's jeep, there was a First Aid Kit with which I stopped the bleeding, but the wound needed suturing which could not be done. What an irony? I have patched-up so many Freedom Fighters' wound during the war, now a month after the liberation I get hurt and there is no one to suture my wounds!

The Family Feud

Anyway, we essentially consumed all day traveling from Thakurgaon to Dhaka. We had left Thakurgaon around 08:00 in the morning; by the time we arrived in Tezgaon in Dhaka it was little past 21:00 Hrs. it took us nearly 13 hours to travel a distance of about 350 km. Coming from the north, my parents' house in Tezgaon comes before Daliah's parents'. The reunion as expected was very emotionally charged. Seeing the brand-new wound on my forehead was not a very welcome scene for my parents. Normally my Mom is a very strong pragmatic person. This was a minor wound, but "if this is what happened today, what else did happen to

Confession of a Terrorist!
Chapter 8   **Longest Month**

you during the past 6+ months?" wailed my mother; Dad as always was hurting inside without visibly expressing his emotion.

About two years prior, I had a very bad motorcycle accident which I most miraculously survived, but took a lot of bruising and abrasions. I was badly hurt; following emergency room care at the Dhaka Medical College Hospital I came home around 20:00 Hrs. and told my mom about it. As strong a person as she was, she immediately assessed my condition that it was not very serious and wanted me to rest. I went to sleep. Dad came home an hour later and was surprised to see that I was already in bed that early. Curiously and being concerned he had asked mom, who defused Dad's anxiety somehow. This evening Dad's voice was not as soft as usual; so after a short nap I woke up and could overhear their conversation; Dad did not come to see me instantly; he was upset to put it mildly. In any event, I was way too tired and I fell asleep again a little later. Then around 02:00 Hrs. he tiptoed into my room along with Mom and was checking my wounds; that woke me up but I was pretending to be in deep sleep. Till today, I vividly recall how agonized he was by seeing my badly bruised body with extensive abrasions all over. Mom had told me the next morning that Dad could not sleep a wink that night, nor could she. So I know how badly Dad was hurting inside.

That Daliah and I got married in Kolkata was not news; Dad knew about it already, perhaps courtesy of Wing Commander Bashar when Dad met him at his hotel after the Victory celebration of 16 December and they accepted her with open arms even though he had the daughter of one of his friends in mind as my future bride. But the problem started a few days later. As is customary in a Bengali society, my parents expected that my newly-wedded wife would be staying in our house with me as a couple. A room was furnished for the newlyweds. Neither was my wife keen about living with me in my parents' house, nor would her mother allow that even over the objection of her father; it seemed that Daliah's father had no say in this matter. Be that as it may, I was 'between a rock and a hard place;' the pressures on me from all the sides were unbearable. The final MBBS examination for us to graduate as medical doctors was scheduled for the first week of March - less than 6 weeks later, and I found it impossible to concentrate in my studies. That I did not have much time to study except occasionally consult the textbook of Medicine over the past 6+ months made it hard to get back into the habit of doing serious studies. Now on top of that, I have to

Confession of a Terrorist!
Chapter 8 Longest Month

deal with the wishes of the wife, the mother-in-law and my parents and try to satisfy them all?! After all, I have to take the exam to get my MBBS degree for which I entered medical college back in summer of 1965. Theoretically, we should have graduated and be doctors in 5 years, by mid-1970; the political unrest started in late 1969 resulting in cancellation of classes and postponement of examinations. Yet, we are not "certified" doctors and we must pass this examination.

To add insult to injury, I started to face other hardships. Having sold off my motorcycle prior to my joining the *Mukti Bahini*, I had to rely on public transportation which became grossly overburdened following the independence. I often walked to and from my parents' home in Tezgaon to the Dhaka Medical College, about 6-7 km, adding physical hardship to my already shattered morale and physique.

As if that was not enough, I came to know that my dear friend and medical school classmate Humayun Kabir, a docile man was executed for no apparent reason by the Pakistani agents on 15 November. He had remained back in the occupied Bangladesh, attended medical college as most of my other classmates did, and took the final MBBS examination to

Confession of a Terrorist!
Chapter 8   **Longest Month**

become a physician. Yet he was slaughtered mercilessly; his corpse was discovered under a culvert near Notre Dame College, our *alma mater*.

Dr. Humayun Kabir, executed by the vicious *Al Bador* the Pakistani paramilitary organization, on 15 November 1971 (source: Google)

Confession of a Terrorist!
Chapter 8   Longest Month

I had mentioned before how astute Mrs. Shirin Bashar was. That there was something wrong in our apparently loving relationship between Daliah and I did not evade the keen observation of Mrs. Bashar; she had suspected that it was not as genuine as it should be or appeared to be. We had briefly talked about it; I had recounted the events in Sector 2 and the circumstances leading to our wedding etc. Knowing that I shall be going through the rigor of my final MBBS examination shortly, very perspicaciously she told me that if things did not go well in Dhaka and I needed some peace and quiet to prepare for my examinations, I could go back to Thakurgaon and stay with them. As discreet as Wing Cmdr. Bashar was, he nodded in agreement without saying anything so as not to make me feel embarrassed the slightest. With their open and earnest invitation in mind, and the fact that I could not study under those situations, I went back to Thakurgaon to put all my efforts uninterrupted by the family feuds [as if it was a rescue mission, to my utter surprise Wing Cmdr. Bashar sent his Command Jeep] a few days before *Eid-ul-Adha*, one of the most important festivals in Bangladesh to commemorate the supposedly aborted sacrifice of a son by his father: Prophet Abraham!

EPILOGUE

I f I have to name the single accomplishment in my life that I am most happy about, it has to be the honor and privilege of serving my motherland in the Liberation War; I tried to serve her the best way I could. Those short 6+ months have also shaped me personally, and affected my life immensely. The experience that I had gained during those times, thanks mostly to the very positive influence of several people whom I considered are my heroes, as well as those who were not, was invaluable. Many people would not have had that experience and personal growth in their lifetime.

What you have read are the description of my own experiences, observations, opinions and comments, and they are solely mine. The purpose was to state the facts as I have seen them, not to offend or lionize anyone – simple statements of facts. I have asked a few questions that naturally came to me. I had invoked my father many times, that's because he had a profound influence in me in not just genetically shaping my physical self, but more importantly my ethical and moral values and my intellect. Like him, I was politically conscious but apolitical; I am that way till this day. I had no party affiliation then or now. It was very refreshing to see that I was not alone, the many Freedom Fighters that I came across were apolitical, simply patriots; and then there were many who had clear and strong affiliations. I have tried to express my gratitude to those who have done acts of kindness to us Bangladeshi Freedom Fighters in general and me personally, irrespective of who they are. It is common in the Bangladeshi community to brand a person either pro-Indian or pro-Pakistani; never have I ever heard of any one as pro-Bengali or pro-Bangladeshi. Lest my expressions of gratitude to my Indian hosts and friends, which in my humble opinion may not even be enough, be interpreted as me being "pro-Indian" let me assure you - yes, I am! Though in my childhood days I sang the national anthem of Pakistan in high-school, I also tagged along with a distant uncle during the Language Movement, revered *Netajee* (still do) and later chanted *Joi Bangla* (Long Live Bangla). Through all these I have always felt that India should have

Confession of a Terrorist!
Epilogue

stayed as one country where all citizens irrespective of their religious beliefs lived as one nation.

My parents have also taught me to act civil, in my critique I have tried to obey that cardinal rule as well; while doing some Internet research on the events leading to the Liberation, I was deeply saddened by the unacceptable language and general lack of civility in some of the forums.

Dad had also educated me to question, see all the sides of an issue and not take anything for gospel truth (except for the Koran, of course!). In honoring his great mentoring, I too have strived to look at the various issues from different perspectives. In the process I'm afraid that I may have made a lot of you unhappy; but making you happy was not my purpose; telling the truth, laying the facts out in the open and critically analyzing to the point of self-criticism no matter how painful that may be was my goal. If I have achieved that, I shall feel accomplished. I am not, and have never been in a popularity contest. These musings of mine are not to gain popular vote, but to challenge the conscious of Bengalis as individuals, and collectively the nation as to look inside ourselves and see if we have any responsibility for our misery; or, to put it in a euphemistic manner: how can we improve.

Epilogue

Physics was my first love and my most favorite law is Newton's third law of motion "To every action there is an equal and opposite reaction." I firmly believe that the law applies to biology and society as well; proofs of that are seen in *karma* and the axiom "those who live by sword die by sword." General Ziaur Rahman became a President by killing, he was killed; the same fate happened to General Khaled Mosharraf and even Sheikh Mujibur Rahman, for he was blasé about the extermination of his political opponents (most notably the cold-blooded execution of the communist leader Shiraz Shikdar) and himself was brutally murdered. This cycle of violence must be stopped; as Mahatma Gandhi had said "an eye for an eye will make the whole world blind."

Having studied cancer most of my life, I can't help but invoke our social problem to compare with this scourge. Fundamental to the formation of cancer is a DNA damage (mutation) that if not repaired propagates through the successive generations of cells, causing the disease. Critical is the repair of the damage; if the DNA lesion is excised and repaired the threat of cancer is removed. Early at the infancy of East Bengal a heinous crime took place that was never corrected. In society as in our body, all wrongs must be corrected, otherwise the 'mutation' in our mind will continue to propagate through our culture resulting in societal apathy or anesthesia to subsequent wrongdoings; essentially, crimes must be punished.

On rare occasions we hear reports of heated debates in some legislative chambers in various countries that descend to fisticuffs, but bar-room style scuffle is even rarer. That the most reprehensible crime of barbaric beating death of the Speaker in the Legislative Chamber was not investigated and the criminal(s) not brought to justice speaks very poorly of us as a society. So, it was no surprise that it took 34 years to bring the killers of the Father of the Nation to justice. My hypothesis may be further substantiated by progressively greater societal apathy and deeper and more generalized anesthesia of not prosecuting the *Razakars* and members of *Al Bodor* and *Al Shams* the Islamic fanatics, who enthusiastically assisted Pakistan government in the genocide of Bengalis, in nearly four decades! The ruthless violence now-a-days rampant in Bangladesh is shocking to say the least; this was not the way Bengalis were 50, or even 20 years ago. So called students are photographed in the front pages of the daily newspapers hacking each other with machetes (*dao*)! Alas, these are the children of the same populace whose cusswords were *"Ghorar Deem"* (literally meaning horse's egg!) or *"dhuttorika"* a word with no meaning or *Shala* (brother-in-law!)!

What has caused the degeneration of this historically docile people to behave in mindless, lawless barbaric manner? Had our social wound in the mid 1950's during the infancy of our new nation been healed - the perpetrators of that scandalous crime brought to justice; I believe we would have evolved into a better society. Yet we are quick to find a scapegoat for all our ills and do not accept responsibility for bad behaviors of ours; only after we can cleanse ourselves then we can hope to isolate and identify the extraneous factors for our misfortune and address those logically and effectively to our benefit.

Assuming that I am correct in my assessment, what are the solutions? I am a physician-scientist, social scientist I am not; within that limitation it is my humble opinion that as a first step we must address the various crimes. Fundamental to solving a problem is to acknowledge it for if we do not accept the fact that we have a problem how can we rectify it? We therefore must admit the wrong-doings. We could adopt the model of The Truth & Reconci-

Epilogue

liation Commission in South Africa; that is one of the approaches that may be helpful in conceding our past errors and healing our wounds for we cannot continue to live on with ever-growing scars in our heart, literally and allegorically. We, as a nation must have zero tolerance for crimes irrespective of who committed it. Judiciary must be independent; justice ought to be blind and swift for justice delayed is justice denied. The power of forgiveness must also not be overlooked, but forgiveness must not be automatic or demanded; a plea to be made to the victim(s) for deserving the compassion and asked for by the truly contrite offenders to complete the healing process on the both sides.

Now, that's a very lofty goal which I am unsure whether it will ever materialize. But one that is equally if not more important is the issue of the Freedom Fighters whose sacrifice made Bangladesh a reality. Every night a Bangladeshi goes to sleep, he/she must remember that it was the sacrifice of those innumerable patriots that have made it possible to keep the shackle of slavery from them. Thus it is a sacred duty of the nation to properly honor them by living up to their dream and the standard they have sacrificed for. Their debt must be repaid not just by taking care of their problems and helping them as best as possible, but also by making the nation what it ought to be – a secular democracy that prospers through liberty, equal justice for all and, a civilized member of the world community …

INTRODUCTION TO CHARACTERS

Akhtar Ahmed *Beer Protik*: Physician in charge of organizing and administering medical care for the Freedom Fighters in Sector 2. He was part of the group who mutinied against the Pakistan Military and was awarded *Beer Pratik* (Exemplary Hero). He retired as a Major in the Bangladesh Army. He had authored two books on Bangladesh Liberation war, one each in Bengali and English.

Ashik, Dr.: A physician who was 3 years' senior to the author. He was a student leader from the left-wing party and was elected as the General Secretary of The Dhaka Medical College Student Union.

Characters

Bashar, Khademul: Commander of Sector 6. At the time of the Liberation war he defected from Pakistan Air Force, was promoted to Wing Commander and following the liberation of Bangladesh became Air Vice-Marshal and Chief of Staff of Bangladesh Air Force. He died in a plane-crash during a celebratory air show on 1 September 1976 on the inauguration day of an air force flight instructors' training school. He received *Beer Uttam* (Superior Hero), the second highest ranking award for valor; also in his honor, the Dhaka base of Bangladesh Air Force was renamed "Bashar Base". While the cause of his plane-crash was never investigated, there were rumors that he was under the influence of alcohol, a very unlikely but gullible story. Given his selflessness, integrity, nonpartisanship and patriotism on one hand and the turbulent political time of the period, sabotage was the more likely explanation.

Chouhan, Major: Commanding Officer of an Indian Border Security Force unit in Sector 2.

Confession of a Terrorist!
Characters

Daliah Salahuddin: My ex-wife; name at birth - Khaleda Haseen (nickname Daliah); she had changed her name to Daliah Salahuddin (after her father Mr. Salahuddin Azad) while entering a Christian Missionary school; and then to Daliah Khaleda Salahuddin. She was a third-year medical student and provided nursing and medical care in Sectors 2 & 6 during the liberation war. Currently, an Internist and Infectious Diseases specialist in Owings Mills, MD, USA.

Danial Islam: My classmate in Technical High School (subsequently named as Intermediate Technical College and now Government Science College & School) in Tezgaon, Dhaka. He had joined Pakistan Army and retired as a Brigadier.

Gafoor: Driver attached to our hospital in Sector 2.

Girendra: My cousin (not blood-related) from my Dad's village

Habul Banerjee: A philanthropist, land-owner expatriate from East Bengal (Bangladesh)

in the State of Tripura (Sector 2) who had most kindly donated part of his land for establishing the medical facility that became the Bangladesh Hospital (Bamboo Hospital)

Hafiz, Mohammed Abdul: My classmate in Dhaka Medical College; currently a practicing pathologist in Atlantic City area in New Jersey, USA.

Islam, Shafi Ahmed: Daliah's cousin

Jeffrey Longu: My classmate and friend in Dhaka Medical College. Jeffrey came to our medical college on a scholarship from the southeast African country of Malawi.

Joydev: My childhood buddy

Kabir, Fazlul Capt: Sub-Sector commander of Dhonpur in Sector 2, my classmate and friend from Notre Dame College.

Kabir, Humayun, Dr.: My classmate in Dhaka Medical College who was slaughtered by the Pakistanis.

Confession of a Terrorist!
Characters

Kashem: A Freedom Fighter in Sector 2, full name Ansar Najmul, currently lives in Canada.

Khaled Mosharraf: Commander of Sector 2. As an officer of the Pakistani Army, he revolted along with other officers and soldiers and established the resistance in Sector 2. Following independence of Bangladesh he was awarded *"Beer Uttam"* and promoted to Brigadier General. Not surprisingly, on 3 November 1975 he staged a military coup, arrested his boss and fellow Freedom Fighter Army Chief of Staff Major General Ziaur Rahman and elevated himself to the rank of a Major General which lasted less than 100 hours as he was killed on 7 November 1975 following a counter-coup.

Khudiram Bose: The first Freedom Fighter to commit an act of violence against the occupying British; he is also famous for going to the gallows with a defiant smile.

Kiron Shankar Debnath: A 4th year student from Dhaka Medical College. Currently he is an anesthesiologist in Plymouth-Norfolk area in Virginia, USA.

Confession of a Terrorist!
Characters

Lulu & Tulu: Sisters Sultana and Sayeeda Kamal (respectively). They were liberal arts students at the University of Dhaka and joined the Resistance to render volunteer nursing care to the freedom fighters in mid-June 1971.

Mahboob, Capt: Sub-Sector Commander of Nirvoypur in Sector 2

Mahmood A. Q. M. (aka Farooq Mahmood): My classmate in Notre Dame College and Dhaka Medical College; currently a practicing ophthalmologist in Dhaka, Bangladesh.

Manzoor: Friend of Shelley and Ulfat, and brother of Maj. Dr. Akhtar Ahmed. He became a commissioned officer in Bangladesh Army.

Matin, 2nd Lt: Newly commissioned officer with the Bangladesh Liberation Army, posted in Sub-Sector 6A under Sq. Ldr. Sadruddin Hossain, younger brother of Capt. Salek of Sector 2.

Confession of a Terrorist!
Characters

Mobin M. A., Dr.: A senior physician who returned from UK, co-founded the Bangladesh Hospital (the bamboo hospital) in Sector 2 along with Dr. Zafrullah Chowdhury.

Mujibur Rahman, Sheikh: Founder of Bangladesh, also known as Sheikh Mujib or *Bongo Bondhu* (Friend of Bengal).

Nazim, Dr.: A physician from Mymensingh Medi-cal College of the University of Dhaka who was one of the first civilian medical doctors to volunteer; following a 2-3 month stay at the Head-Quarter in Melaghor he joined the Bamboo Hospital in Bisramgonj.

Nazrul Islam: An engineer who died of cerebral malaria during the war in Sector 2 while under my care.

Netajee **Shuvash** Chandra Bose: The legendary Freedom Fighter of Indian independence.

Nurul Kader Flt Lt: Sub-Sector Commander in Sector 4. He was one of my High School buddies.

Confession of a Terrorist!
Characters

Podda: Also spelled a Padma, a volunteer nurse in Sector 2, perhaps the only one who had a formal training as a nurse.

Profullo: My childhood friend in my Dad's village

Raton: My childhood buddy and a Freedom Fighter who was killed along with his 3 brothers Makhon, Lucky and Shahar by the Pakistani Military

Roy Choudhury, Dr.: Chief Surgeon at GB Hospital in Agartala, capital of the Indian state of Tripura, Sector 2

Sabita Mondol Biswas: My classmate in Dhaka Medical College, married to an upperclassman Dr. Shonkor Biswas, travelled with Daliah and I to Sector 6. A practicing psychiatrist, she currently lives in UK.

Sadruddin Hossain, Sq. Ldr.: Commander of Sub-Sector 6A. He became Air Vice-Marshal and Chief of Staff of the Bangladesh Air Force.

Confession of a Terrorist!
Characters

Salek Capt: Subsector Commander in Sector 6, my classmate in Notre Dame College, Dhaka. 2nd Lt Matin of Sector 6 was his younger brother.

Selim, Ali Hafiz: My classmate in Dhaka Medical College, medical officer with Capt. Salek. Following the independence, he went to Libya as a medical officer where he and his entire family died in a very tragic auto-accident.

Shelly: Daliah's brother, full name – Syed Mesbahuddin Hashemi.

Shirin: Mrs. Shirin Bashar, wife of Wing Cmdr. Khademul Bashar, Commander of Sector 6.

Shishu: Major Nurul Islam was an important member in the Central Command of the Bangladesh Liberation Army

Sirkar, Mr.: Chief of Indian Red Cross, Shiliguri, West Bengal, Sector 6

Sitara, Begum Capt.: Medical Officer in Sector 2, sister of Capt. Haider also of Sector 2. Currently she lives in USA.

Confession of a Terrorist!
Characters

Snighda *dee*: A physician who was a year senior to me in Dhaka Medical College; one of the most loving and caring persons that I have had the privilege to be acquainted with.

Taher: A soldier, Capt. Akhtar's Batman

Ulfat: The First terrorist I met. He was a friend of Shelly and Manzoor; the three of them left Dhaka to join the Resistance in India.

Zafrullah Chowdhury, Dr.: Along with Dr. Mobin Chowdhury he was a co-founder of the Bangladesh Hospital in Sector 2 in Bisramgonj (the bamboo hospital). He was a stu-dent leader during his Dhaka Medical College days, went to UK and came to India during the liberation war.

Zakia Hussein: A teacher at Eden College, Dhaka who joined us and provided nursing care to our freedom fighters.

Zeenat Yasmin Choudhury: My classmate in Dhaka Medical College and friend.

Confession of a Terrorist!
Characters

Zia-ur Rahman: Commander of Sector 1. He and his troops revolted soon after 25th March, declared the independence of Bangladesh over the radio; became President of Bangladesh and later was killed during a military coup. While he personally lived an austere life, his political actions were controversial. He had clamped-down on corruptions by his opposition party Awami League, yet rehabilitating the assassins of the Father of the Nation – Sheikh Mujibur Rahman. He tweaked with the Constitution to make the country less secular to cozy-up to the Moslem countries, including Pakistan resulting in the upsurge of Islamic fanaticism and religious intolerance towards non-Muslims, especially Hindus.

Zubayer: A 3rd year medical student during the liberation war. He served in Sector 2.

-x-

www.ingramcontent.com/pod-product-compliance
Lightning Source LLC
Chambersburg PA
CBHW060456090426
42735CB00011B/2004